JULIAN J. ROTHBAUM DISTINGUISHED LECTURE SERIES

CONGRESS AND THE INCOME TAX

CONGRESS AND THE INCOME TAX

By
BARBER B. CONABLE, JR.

With A. L. Singleton

UNIVERSITY OF OKLAHOMA PRESS: NORMAN AND LONDON

Library of Congress Cataloging-in-Publication Data

Conable, Barber B.
  Congress and the income tax.

  (Julian J. Rothbaum distinguished lecture series ; v. 2)
  Includes index.
      1. Income tax—Law and legislation—United States—
  History. 2. United States. Congress. House.
  Committee on Ways and Means—History. I. Singleton,
  Arthur L. II. Series.
  KF6369.C66 1989   343.7305'2   88-40542
  ISBN 0-8061-2195-5 (alk. paper) 347.30352

The paper in this book meets the guidelines for permanence and durability of the Committee on Production Guidelines for Book Longevity of the Council on Library Resources, Inc.

CONTENTS

FOREWORD

AMONG THE MANY GOOD THINGS that have happened to me in my life, there is none in which I take more pride than the establishment of the Carl Albert Congressional Research and Studies Center at the University of Oklahoma, and none in which I take more satisfaction than the Center's presentation of the Julian J. Rothbaum Distinguished Lecture Series. The series is a perpetually endowed program of the University of Oklahoma, created in honor of Julian J. Rothbaum by his wife, Irene, and son, Joel Jankowsky.

Julian J. Rothbaum, my close friend since our childhood days in southeastern Oklahoma, has long been a leader in Oklahoma civic affairs. He has served as a Regent of the Uni-

versity of Oklahoma for two terms and as a State Regent for
Higher Education. In 1974 he was awarded the University's
highest honor, the Distinguished Service Citation, and in
1986 he was inducted into the Oklahoma Hall of Fame.

The Rothbaum Lecture Series is devoted to the themes of
representative government, democracy and education, and
citizen participation in public affairs, values to which Julian J.
Rothbaum has been committed throughout his life. His life-
long dedication to the University of Oklahoma, the state, and
his country is a tribute to the ideals to which the Rothbaum
Lecture Series is dedicated. The books comprising the series
make an enduring contribution to an understanding of American democracy.

CARL B. ALBERT

*Forty-sixth Speaker
of the
United States House of Representatives*

PREFACE

MANY THINGS HAVE HAPPENED between my delivery of the Carl Albert Lectures at the University of Oklahoma in 1985 and the publication of this book based on what I said then.

First, three years have passed. Memory is vapor, soon dissipated. Legislation, the subject of my lectures, is written on the wind. The claim can be made that the book is no longer timely. But legislatures are institutions of tradition, and traditions endure. I believe this to be a book about Congress, an important institution to Americans, rather than a book about the course of income tax legislation. Legislating taxation affecting the American people is a sensitive business, and so when Congressmen work in this special way, they tend to reveal more about themselves, their thought patterns, and their institutional work habits than when they are voting on more-neutral, more-accepted bills relating to defense, or agriculture, or national parks.

Next, my own life has changed since I gave those lectures. Then I was pleasantly and comfortably retired after twenty years in the House of Representatives, with much time on my hands, fresh and rewarding memories on which I could easily draw. I was confident that I could entertain young minds eager for a glimpse of the world of public service. Shortly after I gave the lectures, a call from the Secretary of the Treasury plunged me into a new world far from the subject of the lectures with which I was so familiar. I was chosen, and have now served for two years, as President of the World Bank, a development institution in the front line of the battle against global poverty. My vivid memories of the Ways and Means Committee have faded, and I read my old journals about its daily work with nostalgia for the past and surprise that I have become so involved once again in a new preoccupation.

And last, tax legislative events have had surprising turns since I spoke. Then, I was profoundly skeptical about the possibilities of a 1986 Tax Act. The Act that emerged a year after the lectures flew in the face of what I thought were reasonable expectations. Strong men broke the patterns I had described in my lectures and forced me into the reassessments that appear for the first time in this book. I am not chagrined by this, but it did delay the end product because it required me to analyze events in which I had not participated.

But this talk about the passage of time and new legislation should not obscure the unchanging reality of Congress, the main subject of this book. We Americans love to call it a human institution. It is never more human than when Congressmen gingerly take up a tax bill, pour their political art into it, argue and compromise, participate and point with pride or dismay, and finally do their duty as they see it, aware that only Congress can determine how and to what degree the people will support their government and its programs.

I would like especially to thank my friend and collaborator, A. L. ("Pete") Singleton, former Chief of Staff of the Ways and Means Committee Minority, for his review, organization, and scholarly additions to the text of my lectures.

Barber B. Conable, Jr.

Washington, D.C.
September, 1988

CONGRESS AND THE INCOME TAX

CHAPTER 1

A FORMER CONGRESSMAN'S
BACKWARD LOOK

EVERYBODY PICKS ON CONGRESS. Hardly anyone will say a laudatory word about the institution. Conversely, finding an unkind cut is easy. One of Mark Twain's comes quickly to mind: "It could probably be shown by facts and figures that there is no distinctly native American criminal class except Congress." He made his point through exaggeration, but he made his point.

When one stops to think about it—and as a former member of Congress, I have thought about it many times—there is something very worrisome about the fact that the best known observations of our national legislature are terribly pejorative. In thinking about it, I also have to confess that I share some of the responsibility for that kind of view. Often during my two decades as an insider, especially on occasions when I disagreed with a majority of my colleagues on some issue, I would call Congress, with great satisfaction, a craven collective. These were passing feelings with me, I should emphasize. Congress is never as bad as Twain alleged, and not always as cowardly as I occasionally charged.

Ironically, because Congress is a collective, sometimes it is seen as craven, is often the butt of jokes, and is usually rated low in public estimation according to most opinion polls. The irony lies in the radically different way the electorate sees Congress as an institution and its members as their institutional representatives. By and large, they love their own members of Congress. Just look at election results! Incumbents are reelected with startling frequency. In recent years, the rate of incumbency return has been above 95 percent. Of course, not all constituents love their representatives. However, most do. So there is a situation in which American people praise their representatives individually and condemn them collectively.

America's founders designed it that way. They created a huge, representative body, largely reactive, slow to respond to hues and cries, anything but monolithic. Our Congress is a truly unique institution. Based to a great extent on the English Parliament, it bears some resemblance to other national legislatures. It is, though, different in many respects from each of them. The income tax structure, which Congress has produced, also is not precisely like any other. Even as it has been changed, with some frequency, it has remained one-of-a-kind. And like its parent, the legislature, it also remains the object of constant protest and complaint. Both our income tax and our national legislature were tailored originally—and have been subjected to alterations periodically—to fit their constituencies. As voters and as taxpayers, we have asked, in effect, for what we have received in both instances.

At the outset of this discussion—and it seems that I have a very long way to go from here—perhaps I had better introduce myself, because what I say is certainly conditioned by my experience and my role in the House of Representatives. I walked into this role without what many critics would consider an adequate preparation. Before I was elected to Congress, I was a country lawyer. Now, I am mindful of what is said about country lawyers (that after you shake hands with one, you should count your fingers), but, nevertheless, I was a lawyer and I did live and practice in rural, upstate New York. I had a one-man office and an unsophisticated clientele.

In recent years, I may have assumed the title, but clearly not the arts, of the political scientist. I have never become one of those scholarly analysts who can tell you, *ad infinitum*, all the details of government. Most members come to Congress as generalists, and remain so. Our national legislature never has drawn specialists to Washington; virtually all of us who have been elected were sent to Congress primarily as spokespersons for folks back home. We were supposed to bring a citizen's horse sense to central government, to have and to exercise the judgment that can warn governmental experts when they are getting too far away from the people. That, essentially, is the kind of perspective that I bring to this subject.

I should emphasize that my fundamental viewpoint is that of a congressman, and I am, in many ways, a creature of the House of Representatives. It provided for me a friendly (most of the time) environment, and I grew to love the institution. The Senate is, as we creatures of the House are wont to say, the other body. I used to tell my constituents (and others who inquired about my occupation) that the Senate, which met way down at the other end of the Capitol, was a land I rarely visited and for which I took no responsibility. In truth, of course, I worked closely with members of that other body, especially those who served on the Finance Committee, the Senate counterpart to Ways and Means. We met often in conference committees, where differences between House and Senate versions of legislation are reconciled. But the House, and the business of the House, consumed virtually the lion's share of my time throughout my legislative career. It demanded almost all of my energy and my attention. And I must confess, I liked the job.

My work in the House was centered on committees to which I was assigned. My major service was with the Committee on Ways and Means, but I also spent a few years with the committees on Science and Technology, Standards of Official Conduct, House Administration, and Budget. Service on the Ways and Means Committee is different in many respects from that on other House committees. It has had broader jurisdiction than most. It also deals with politically sensitive, "pocketbook" issues, not only income taxation but social insurance, welfare, foreign trade, the public debt of the United States, and other non-income taxes affecting both individuals and corporations.

Membership on this committee is highly selective. Both political parties in the House make an effort to choose only those members who have relatively "safe" seats, on the theory that they can make tough decisions and survive. That is to say, they should be able to cast votes in the national interest, without losing their jobs in elections that are based largely on narrowly defined, parochial issues. My career in Congress was influenced not only by my background and by my committee assignments, but by my choice of political party. Let me tell you that this was a factor of no small dimension.

Many Americans forget, or remain blissfully unaware, that Congress is run by political parties. The House of Representatives has been under control of the Democratic Party for fifty of the past fifty-four years. The Senate has changed hands in this period, but not the House. Since 1932, there have been twenty-seven congresses. In two of them, the Eightieth (1947–1949) and the Eighty-third (1953–1955), Republicans had a majority in the House. For the past sixteen congresses (thirty-two straight years), the Democratic Party has been in charge.

My position in the House, then, was conditioned by the fact that during my entire career I was in the minority. As the Republican leader on the Ways and Means Committee, I never could go between two places in a straight line. I always had to try to lay ambushes for my majority colleagues and to achieve what I could through indirection. Without even a remote hope of getting enough votes to dominate, one resorts to whatever stratagems one can find and use. In my own case, however, there was little satisfaction to be derived from devious dealings. I much preferred to move in a straight line, and I frankly did not like being forced to take a circuitous route. This was a major factor, I must confess, in my decision to leave Congress and go on to other things. Twenty years in a minority position finally took its toll.

Despite my minority status, I will admit to being involved in what I hope was a responsible way in some critical matters before the House. This was, in part, because I was a member of the Republican leadership of the House for fourteen years, and, as such, had the privilege of representing my party at White House strategy meetings. That White House association sometimes gave me an influence beyond the voting groups in the House with which I was associated.

I was the ranking Republican on the Ways and Means Committee for eight years, an unusually long tenure. There was a big turnover on Ways and Means during my very early years on the committee, but not so in more recent times. Some members on my side of the aisle have now served eight or more years on the committee and still rank sixth and seventh in seniority. That reflects a new congressional stability, and a much higher percentage of victories for incumbents, even those with controversial assignments. Being in a minority, not able to put one's political position to direct legislative use, tended in my case to promote greater interest in the mechanics of legislation, how processes come to be. Perhaps my frustrations explain my recurrent efforts to bring about procedural and substantive changes. I was an aggressive participant in many tax, trade, and social-security reforms.

I have been viewed generally as a conservative, but I agree with Edmund Burke that any conservative worthy of the name should do some systems maintenance work. He didn't use those exact words. He said, in effect, that reforms can have differing meanings depending on timing: an early reform is an accommodation with a friend, a late reform a capitulation to an enemy. He also said that all government is founded on compromise and barter. As a believer, I tried to participate in systems maintenance work early on. Happily that led, in turn, to some interesting roles, despite my minority status. Enough, though, about my perspective. By now, I think, the way I have come is clear—as a citizen participant conditioned by reality, not a political analyst or scientist—to the subject of Congress and the income tax.

Let's move now to an overall, non-technical view of the tax code itself, with attention first to the general perception that people seem to have of taxes and tax reform. Most polls have told us—over and over—that a tax on income is the most un-popular tax. Sixty to 65 percent of the American people have identified income tax as the one that they really hate. I don't believe there is any mystery about that. Taxes always have been a major issue, a rubbing point if you will, between gov-ernment and the people, and that will continue as long as representatives have to raise as much money as government is spending. Among all taxes, the income tax is the big one.

It is visible, and therefore much of the animosity toward taxation as a whole attaches to the income tax in particular. There are other taxes, of course, and some of them have rather unfortunate effects and incidences. For example, there is the social-security tax. President Reagan, and others before him, have declared it an outrage that some Americans, who are at or near the poverty line, are paying 10 percent of their income in federal taxes. About 7 percent of that total is paid into social security. It's a payroll tax. Each employee now pays 7.51 percent of the first dollar he or she earns through the FICA tax, which supports the Old Age, Survivors, and Dis-ability Insurance trust funds. The employee gets a lot of pro-tection—and ultimately some cash benefits—in return for those payments, so it is certainly not lost money. However, it is a substantial tax outlay, and regressive at that. Of that 10 percent of income purportedly paid in federal taxes by many poor Americans, less than 3 percent is paid in income taxes. But it's all withheld from the same paycheck, and the wage earner may not know which bee in the swarm is sting-ing him or her. Clearly and understandably, the income tax draws most complaints. Usually this is what is meant in talk about tax reform.

A reality worth noting is that, to a remarkable degree throughout the life of this country, negative traditions of American politics have run strong. By negative traditions, I mean that people have always tended to be against, rather than for, something or someone. That is what activates them politically. That such is the case doesn't bother me. Frankly, I think that people's being dissatisfied with the way the system works is a good idea. Dissatisfaction is the natural precursor to doing something about it, to making improvements.

One of the reasons that America has been a dynamic society is that its citizens have tended to focus on the negative, and to resent this or that exercise of government power. That also is one of the reasons we have not cast our lot with one national party exclusively, but have tended to shift our collective support for the presidency back and forth from one party to another. Sooner or later, we are always against people in power, always yearning for and actively seeking a different sort of leadership.

These negative traditions of American politics have attached very strongly to the tax system, which suffers chronically from something called the "man bites dog" syndrome. What usually makes news is exceptional behavior. The standard example of the phenomenon is that when a man bites a dog, it's news, and someone writes a story about it. If all a person knew about the relationship between men and dogs is what is read in that news story, the reader might think that men went around biting dogs, when, in fact, the reality is quite different. The tax system lends itself to the syndrome. Finding a millionaire who, for some reason, doesn't pay taxes is always possible. That is the tax policy equivalent of a man's biting a dog. That becomes the focal point. That's what makes news, and generates the enthusiasm for reform.

Obviously, what makes news is not always what really happens, least of all in the world of tax policy. For instance, in terms of wealth, the top 10 percent of the people pay almost 50 percent of aggregate income taxes collected. The next lower 40 percent of the people, again in terms of wealth, pay about 40 percent of aggregate income taxes collected. And the other 50 percent of the population pays the remaining 10 percent of aggregate income taxes collected. Those are only approximations, but they establish an appropriate profile for a progressive tax system.

This doesn't mean that people who are poor aren't every bit as unhappy about taxes as people who are well-to-do. It also does not mean the middle class pays *all* the taxes. But it does run counter to a perception most people have about income tax. Many of them think the rich don't pay *any* taxes. They assume that what they have read in the paper, about a few millionaires who do not pay taxes for one reason or another, is the reality of the tax system, and that makes them unhappy. The tax system then draws the full brunt of their negative view. In a democracy perception sometimes is politically more real than reality. As a result, legislators respond to the pressures of democracy, not to statistical analysis.

This raises interesting questions. For example, could another income tax system, particularly one that has a level rate, possibly raise as much money from the top 10 percent of the people, which generally are those who earn above $60,000 or $70,000 now? Maybe we'll know the answer one of these days, if Americans ever get what so many have wanted: an absolutely "flat" tax. However, for the foreseeable future, we do have to deal with the "man bites dog" syndrome that leads people to view taxes much more skeptically than perhaps they would or should if they looked at the figures. I will acknowledge that this set of concepts is a little more complicated than I am making it here, but I will attempt to elaborate later on.

The second thing about the tax system that people don't like is its complexity. There is no question about it, it has become increasingly complicated. When Jimmy Carter called the income tax a disgrace to the human race, he really was talking more about complexity than anything else. On April 14, taxpayers view complexity as unfairness. That is why tax reform is a change every recent president has pushed. Presidents seeking the favor of the taxpaying public know what they're doing. President Ronald Reagan not only knew what he was doing in terms of gaining favor with the taxpaying public, but he knew how to do what his predecessors only wanted to do: he actually got major tax reform.

The normal definition of tax reform, as far as the average American is concerned, can be stated as follows: "I am paying too much tax because somebody else isn't paying enough." That's the heart of the fairness question. Polls show very clearly that people really believe the income tax system is unfair. Some, to distill tax reform, might put it this way: "You have got to catch those people who are not paying their fair share of the tax, so that we can bear a more appropriate share of the total burden." Fairness has to do with the vantage point of the viewer. If you have ever claimed a deduction, that is fair. If you have not claimed a deduction, it's a giveaway. In sum, the general perception of our tax code is that it is unfair, that it's complex, that others are not paying enough, and that it is, in fact, a personal tragedy for the hardworking taxpayer. Now, how did we get to this point? Americans started with a simple tax. That's what people wanted and they got it originally. What happened? The answer, of course, is that people changed their collective minds as the years went by and the conditions of American life were altered.

If there is one thread that will run through this entire commentary, it is the thread of compromise. Congress is a collective, a very large one—535 ambitious achievers, gathered together for decision-making purposes in one building, the United States Capitol. If there were no compromises, no meetings of these 535 fertile minds, Congress would be forever immobilized, unable to agree on any legislation whatsoever, doomed to listen eternally to the drone of its members' voices, each offering its own solution, totally without resolution. As bad as some of our laws may be, surely none of us would prefer a completely non-productive national legislature.

So it is with tax policy, a major preoccupation of Congress. If there were no tax compromises, there never would have been a Sixteenth Amendment in the first place. We might still be relying on tariffs for federal revenues, and, as momentarily tempting as that might seem to some fiscal conservatives, the reality is that we simply could not survive as a nation on that revenue potential.

Now, on the theory, and with the hope, that I have satisfactorily introduced the subject and established my credentials and perspective for discussing it, let me describe briefly the matters that I intend to pursue in substantial depth. First, I think some rather extensive elaborations on the Ways and Means Committee might be helpful. I plan to look at its history and its place in today's Congress, as well as some of the personalities who have guided it in recent years. And I will, of course, be reflecting in this process on my own participation in the life and work of the Ways and Means Committee. Next, I plan to examine in much greater detail the evolution of America's federal income tax system, starting from its very beginnings. Third, I will spend some time on a part of the tax policy equation that all too often is neglected: spending as well as getting money to run the national government. If Americans do not address this part of our fiscal universe, we simply cannot begin to understand the whole. Finally, I think dealing with our representative government as it has developed and as it exists today is appropriate. Congress and the income tax become much easier to understand, I think, against this broad backdrop.

CHAPTER 2

THE COMMITTEE ON WAYS AND MEANS

THE COMMITTEE ON WAYS AND MEANS is the oldest standing committee of the Congress. It was established first on an ad hoc basis in 1789, when a Federal member from Pennsylvania, Mr. Thomas Fitzsimons, stated during a debate on federal finances that ". . . revenue of $3 million in specie will enable us to provide every supply necessary to support the Government, and pay the interest and installments on the foreign and domestic debt." He added: "If we wish to have more particular information on these points, we ought to appoint a Committee of Ways and Means. . . ." Mr. Fitzsimons made a formal motion to that effect, it was agreed to, and, not surprisingly, he was appointed chairman of the new committee.

Ways and Means deals with sums considerably in excess of three million dollars these days, but it is still at the same old stand, to some extent, trying to find enough money to keep the government running. The ad hoc committee, I should note, did not last very long, but Ways and Means was revived a few years later as a permanent standing committee, under the chairmanship of William Smith, of South Carolina, and charged with the following duty:

> to take into consideration all such reports of the Treasury Department, and all such propositions, relative to the revenue, as may be referred to them by the House; to inquire into the state

of the public debt, of the revenue, and of the expenditures; and to report, from time to time, their opinion thereon."

In its early days, this committee had responsibility to oversee not only authorizations of money, but appropriations of money, plus banking and currency operations. The jurisdiction was so broad that one historian commented about the committee: "It seemed like an Atlas bearing on its shoulders all the business of the House." "Atlas" was not relieved of any part of his burden until 1865, when Congress reorganized in an effort to deal more efficiently with financial demands caused by the Civil War. In the reorganization process, control over appropriations was transferred to a Committee on Appropriations, and other segments of responsibility were handed over to a new Committee on Banking and Currency.

Even though it gave up some jurisdiction, Ways and Means remained a powerful committee because of its remaining authority—and also because its chairman was automatically the ad hoc majority floor leader of the House. Several generations later, the committee's power was increased further when Democratic members of the committee were given the job of appointing Democratic members of all other House committees. One can imagine the enormous authority and influence such Ways and Means Democrats, especially the chairmen, were able to exert throughout most of this century. Except for four years when Republicans had a House majority, the Chairman of the Ways and Means Committee could be called, fairly, the most powerful member next to the Speaker. This power declined rather sharply and abruptly in the 1970s, and I will shortly discuss that change in detail.

Throughout its history, many famous Americans have served on the Ways and Means Committee. There have been seven presidents, including Millard Fillmore, a fellow New Yorker, and eight vice-presidents, including Vice-president George Bush. I had the pleasure of serving with George Bush during the Ninetieth and Ninety-first Congresses—from 1967 to 1971. We sat in adjoining seats, far down the seniority line, among the most junior members, and I profited from his brilliance. Together we entered the sometimes arcane world of Ways and Means, often straining to hear what was being said, in the distance, at the center of the committee. The chairman and the ranking Republican at that time were Wilbur Mills of Arkansas and John Byrnes of Wisconsin. Both men were extremely bright, and between them had a knowledge of the Internal Revenue Code that was not only admirable but intimidating. One problem for junior members, seated at a distance, was that both Mills and Byrnes spoke softly, and, for all practical purposes, to one another, as they conducted committee business. There would be a great deal of muttering at the center of the dais, then Mills would raise his voice briefly to ask: "Can we agree to that?" On occasion, some time and some brash questioning from the lower ranks were needed to find out precisely what had been agreed upon.

Over the years I rose in seniority, moved closer to the center, and was able to hear much better. In the process, I served really on three different Ways and Means committees. There was, first, the Wilbur Mills committee, then the Al Ullman committee, and finally the Dan Rostenkowski committee. Each of these chairmen worked in distinctly different ways and created a distinctly different kind of committee. They were illustrative of the reality that policy is made by people and that people make a great difference.

THE MILLS COMMITTEE

When Wilbur Mills was the chairman, working on the Ways and Means Committee was a most fortunate opportunity for a freshman Republican, or a very young Republican. George Bush was just junior to me because he was a freshman and I was a sophomore. Strangely, Wilbur Mills worried as much about our votes as he did about the votes of senior Democrats on the committee. He wanted to stretch the tent so that everybody could get in it. He wanted to bring his bills to the floor with consensus support. At that time, the committee had twenty-five members, and he preferred a vote of at least twenty-three to two to show clearly that the committee strongly supported whatever measure was brought forth.

Mills was a legislative leader in the old-fashioned sense of the word; he gave his entire attention to the process. He was a psychologist, too, who knew what we thought before we knew it ourselves—a brilliant man, and quite devious. He also presided over a political function of considerable importance because that was part of committee and congressional life at that time. As I mentioned earlier, Democrats on the Ways and Means Committee, and usually there were fifteen of them to our Republican ten, also served as their party's committee on committees. They were elected by the Caucus (which includes all Democrats in the House) to the Ways and Means Committee, and then they appointed all their colleagues to other committees. Now, that is a political function of considerable magnitude. As you know, one's effectiveness in the House is frequently judged by the type of committee assignment one has. This meant that the Ways and Means Democrats came to reflect the power structure of the Democratic party in the House. They were people with a following.

To illustrate that, one year Omar Burleson, a Texas Democrat and then chairman of the House Administration Committee, with twenty years of seniority, decided to give up his status to seek a seat, as a freshman, on the Ways and Means Committee. I recall that vividly because, as a matter of fact, that was the year I joined the committee. In the contest for the next open Ways and Means spot, Omar was defeated by one vote in the Caucus by Jack Gilbert, a New York City congressman. Texas, as a result, did not have a representative at that time among the Democrats on the Ways and Means Committee. Oil-drilling interests were desolate. Gerald Ford, who was then Minority Leader of the House, took note of this situation and decided that the time had come to take the unprecedented step of putting a freshman Republican on the committee, and that choice turned out to be George Bush, of Houston. The Republican Leader wanted to show the people of Texas that the Republican party cared about Texas, even if the Democrats did not.

Of course, Omar Burleson did join the committee the next time around. What is interesting is that Omar was willing to risk his standing in the House to try to get on the Ways and Means Committee and to fight as tough and persistent a fight as he did. He served on the committee for six years. He was a distinguished older man, with high rank elsewhere, who came aboard late in his career as a freshman member because Ways and Means service was real status, both politically and legislatively.

Well, that kind of thing was important to Wilbur Mills. He was able to translate status, knowledge, and power into the kind of respect that led callow youths to avoid challenging his bills on the floor of the House. He was not an authoritarian. He was smooth as silk, but people knew he was not to be trifled with. Because Mills wanted it that way, because it served his purposes, Ways and Means was, then, a consensus committee in every sense of the word. This made it exceptionally interesting to watch the interplay on that committee between Mills and Byrnes, the ranking Republican.

Wilbur Daigh Mills was born in 1909, in the little town of Kensett, Arkansas. His father was a well-to-do businessman in the community, and there was no "log cabin" in his background. He attended nearby Hendrix College, and then went on to Harvard Law School. Despite his Cambridge training and his obvious skill in tax law, he appeared to relish the deceptive role of country lawyer, a position he actually held for a very few years in Searcy, Arkansas, between his graduation from Harvard in 1933 and his election to Congress in 1938.

John William Byrnes perhaps was not generally as well known as was Wilbur Mills, but his contributions to the legislative process and to the achievements of the Committee on Ways and Means were well known by close observers. Larry

Woodworth, a long-time chief of the Joint Tax Committee staff, which serves both Ways and Means and Senate Finance, once said: "When I come to the Ways and Means table to talk about some new tax proposal, I always 'key' on John Byrnes. His reaction is the most critical in determining the way I tackle the issue." John Manley, a Brookings Institution scholar who wrote a book, *The Politics of Finance*, in 1970, observed:

> Mills and Byrnes together, not just Mills alone, are responsible for the way the Committee goes about its business. Far from being cut off from influence in the committee, the Republicans feel that because of Mills and Byrnes they have as much say if not more than the Democrats.

John Byrnes came from Green Bay, Wisconsin, where he was born in 1913. Two years after gaining his law degree from the University of Wisconsin in 1938, he was elected to the state senate, and four years after that, he was a member of Congress. He joined Ways and Means in 1947, and he and Mills served together, often side-by-side, for the next quarter of a century. They often disagreed, but when they were united on a measure, it usually carried both House and Senate by large majorities. John Byrnes died recently, and his death was a national loss, as well as a personal loss to his friends.

The committee relationship between these two men was fascinating, as it would be in any institution favored by their presence. John Byrnes was as direct and intellectually honest as Wilbur was elusive. John was, in a way, the first sergeant of the Ways and Means company. An issue would come up, and John would plunge head on into the heart of it with both arms flailing. Not a bit politic, but very direct and forceful, he would get the committee formed in line and marching off down the road. When he saw that the committee had decided what it wanted to do, thanks to John Byrnes' honest and persuasive ministrations, the company commander—Wilbur Mills—would appear out of the bushes, position himself at the head of the column, and the committee consensus would become the Mills bill.

An effective military organization needs both a company commander and a first sergeant, and in the Ways and Means Committee this also constituted very effective leadership. Yet it had an interesting side effect. Since Wilbur wanted a consensus committee, since John Byrnes provided a lot of the momentum within the committee, and since Wilbur was a legislative psychologist who waited for the committee to make up its mind and then positioned himself at the head of the column, the result was that the Ways and Means Committee came to have a consensus that was much more conservative than was the case with the majority of the Democratic party in the House. The committee was viewed as having a life of its own, to the dismay of liberal Democrats.

If Wilbur Mills was going to worry about what Barber Conable and George Bush thought about something, and would try to stretch the legislative tent to get them under it, along with the most senior of Democrats—such as Louisiana's Hale Boggs, Kentucky's John Watts, and others—then quite obviously the consensus that resulted was not going to be the same kind of liberal consensus that characterized the majority of the majority party. And that in itself was eventually enough to doom Wilbur's leadership, because the majority party understandably came to feel that it had an absolute right to do what it finally did—that is, to impose political accountability on an institution that had come to have a life of its own.

If the system were to function as the majority had a right to expect it to function, then the type of performance given by Ways and Means had to be changed, and it was. The major change was taking away the assignment of Ways and Means Democrats as a "committee on committees," with, in effect, the authority to appoint other House Democrats to seats on other committees. This was a great loss of power for our committee's Democrats, especially for the chairman. Another big change was increasing the numerical size of the committee and, in the process, adding a disproportionate number of Democrats to assure that a committee plurality would reflect more tellingly the sentiment of most Democrats in the House as a whole.

Wilbur Mills, in his heyday, had a remarkable record of success on the floor of the House. His bills almost always passed. They passed, not because he was authoritarian, not because he abused his position as the chairman of the committee on committees, but because he worried about winning—always. He would disappear from our view for two or three days before we were about to disgorge a bill from the Ways and Means Committee. He would be out on the floor of the House talking and listening, holding an envelope, on the back of which he had written names of key Democrats. He would go around making sure that these influential members were able to accept this or that provision of the bill. He might come back the day before we were to vote it out of committee and say: "Fellows, we have got to change the bill. We are going to have trouble." And he would suggest this or that potential change. In other words, he went through an informal democratic process to be sure that he was not going to be defeated on the floor with respect to any detail.

Well, Wilbur eventually fell from his position of great authority. His friends recall that with sorrow. I am not one of those who tells disparaging stories about Wilbur Mills. I have always questioned whether he really was an alcoholic, but he clearly was having trouble with his back and taking painkillers, conventional and unconventional, and I think he finally underwent some kind of temporary personality alteration. Parenthetically, I might note that Wilbur is perfectly fine now. He has been associated with a prestigious Washington law firm, and remains active. I wish him well and admire his legendary leadership. As I look back, his work was never affected, as far as I could tell. I never saw him drunk or thought him uncharacteristically ineffective. He cooperated with the effort to impose political accountability on this committee, which had become so independent during his tenure. In effect, he voluntarily retired as chairman, and, as a result, he was replaced in 1974 by the next ranking Democrat, the late Al Ullman, a very gentlemanly, serious, and earnest person from Oregon.

THE ULLMAN COMMITTEE

Al came out of the tradition of consensus, but he had been ordered by the Caucus and the leaders of the Democratic party to change the way in which the Ways and Means Committee functioned. Along with Mills, he concurred with the move, in 1975, to take the "committee on committees" function away from Ways and Means Democrats and give it instead to a steering committee in which the Speaker would have a much stronger hand. This was part of the process of imposing political accountability.

The Ways and Means Committee also was given a larger membership as a consequence of the Legislative Reorganization Act of 1974. Total committee membership went from twenty-five to thirty-seven and assumed subcommittee structure, something not done until that time. As part of the Wilbur Mills consensus, all of our decisions had been made *en banc*. Each member knew all there was to know, or all he or she was willing to absorb, about every issue that came up. When a bill was being developed, the entire committee would sit down, review options, and spend whatever time was necessary to reach a consensus. The process might take weeks or months, and no detail seemed too small to leave either to chance or staff decision-making.

Control of the process is much easier if there are subcommittees. If there are pressure points within the committee where certain types of legislation are generated, then although members continue to be technically equal, some become more equal than others. Where there is a separate staff for each subcommittee, that staff becomes expert in one particular, narrow area. Members themselves may no longer take individual responsibility for everything on which they are voting. Instead, they may give credibility to the expertise of the specialized subcommittee, which holds separate hearings rather than the old *en banc* procedure. All of a sudden, on Ways and Means, we had not just one large kingdom, but six separate satrapies or principalities as well. Princes reported to the king, of course, but authority was diffused, along with knowledge about the differently generated bills.

Another big adjustment for Ways and Means came with a loss of jurisdiction. As a result of the Reorganization Act of 1974 (a brainchild largely of Congressman Richard Bolling of Missouri, who later became chairman of the Rules Committee), Ways and Means was relieved of certain programs that were paid out of general revenues, not specific trust fund taxes. The largest program in this category was Medicaid, the medical assistance program for the needy, sort of a welfare counterpart to Medicare. Medicaid jurisdiction shifted to what is now the Energy and Commerce Committee, which also has a health subcommittee. Part B of Medicare, the portion covering payment for physicians' fees, also is largely paid for out of general revenues, so jurisdiction over this program is now shared between Ways and Means and Energy and Commerce. Also dropped from Ways and Means care and feeding was the revenue-sharing program developed during the Nixon administration as part of the new federalism. I had a major part in enacting this program, and still think it was a good idea for its time. That time has passed, however, and the program no longer exists.

One of the biggest changes at Ways and Means was in staff. There not only were many more people around to handle each subcommittee's business, but their overall influence rose. Subcommittees often met concurrently, with the result that members, torn by competing demands for their time and attention (since they served on more than one subcommittee), began relying increasingly on staffs for advice and guidance. This was a sea change for the committee, a dramatic shift in legislative approach. Thus, Al Ullman inherited a command that had been substantially altered, and weakened.

There was no way he could have paralleled Mills' record, even if he had so desired.

Al Ullman was a substantive man. He was interested in the tax law. His word was good. He was a kind colleague and a good leader. I always felt a little sorry for him for having to try to change a committee, so accustomed to consensus, into a committee that would be more accountable to the majority in his party. Of course, we Republicans all kicked and screamed. Ullman did as good a job as he could. He was very earnest. He would say, "I have grave reservations" about this, or "I have grave reservations" about that. Members had a good time with that one. I remember we used to say, "Al Ullman has so many grave reservations, he must be registered in every cemetery in the country."

Al made the mistake of being too substantive. He felt that one of his responsibilities was to try to lead, and he got the wonderful idea that a consumption tax, a value-added tax, was an idea whose time had come. His constituents did not universally share that view. In Oregon, he represented the whole eastern three-quarters of the state. There was no town in his district that had more than twenty thousand people. His idea was not appreciated at home. The people there had twice knocked down, on referendum, a proposal for a state sales tax. But Al still thought a national value-added tax would be a wonderful idea, though it is a form of sales tax. In no time at all, he had a new opponent going around small-town Oregon saying: "Guess what your friendly local congressman wants to have: a national sales tax. And after you folks have twice voted down the state sales tax."

Al also did not benefit from President Carter's early concession statement following the November, 1980, general election. When Carter acknowledged defeat almost as soon as it seemed apparent, many people on the West Coast were still standing in line to vote. Both his strong campaign for a value-added tax and Carter's early concession were credited with Al Ullman's defeat in 1980. There also was some talk to the effect that demands on him, as chairman of the Ways and Means Committee, kept him in Washington too much and thus prevented him from spending enough time in his home district. Whatever the reasons, he did lose his seat only six years after assuming command of the committee. Ullman was succeeded by Dan Rostenkowski of Illinois.

THE ROSTENKOWSKI COMMITTEE

There was some speculation among members that Rostenkowski would elect to remain on the House leadership ladder, which normally leads to the Speakership. Dan was a deputy majority whip at the time, and it was clear he could not serve both as chairman of Ways and Means and as an active member of the top House Democratic leadership. That might have been possible in the past, but current caucus rules would not permit it. Knowing of Dan Rostenkowski's apparent desire to become Speaker some day, many were surprised when he took the helm of the committee. In some respects, that appeared counter to his career pattern up until then.

Dan was not placed on this committee primarily because he was interested in the substantive problems the tax law had to offer. He was Chicago Mayor Richard Daley's representative on the Ways and Means Committee. He benefited from his relationship to Mayor Daley through a direct telephone line to his congressional office. The Cooke County delegation used to meet there regularly. Mayor Daley was a bright-enough, sophisticated-enough man to know that if he wanted to project his power into the Congress of the United States, the best way to do it was through an agent on the Ways and Means Committee who could participate in the assignment of young Democratic congressmen from the Midwest to productive committee posts. That is why Dan was there in the first place. He rarely stayed in meetings for long periods of time until he became the leader. Even then he appeared to become the leader with some reluctance.

I don't want to go into all of my own suspicions about why

he became the Chairman of the Ways and Means Committee, other than that he never had to worry about surviving in south Chicago. They eat Republicans there. Now, Dan Rostenkowski has taken a bum rap in some academic circles. He really is a bright man. Let's put it this way. He knows what he needs to know to get done what he wants to get done. Intellectually, he is perfectly capable of understanding the most complicated problems of tax law. He has demonstrated that clearly by now. He just isn't all that interested in the intricacies of tax law. So, he tends to respond to the political opportunities of tax legislation. He took a committee that had been in transition under Al Ullman and put it firmly in the accountability column to the Democratic party of the House.

Ironically, when Rostenkowski assumed the chairmanship of the Ways and Means Committee in 1980, a coalition of conservatives had taken over control of the House, and yet he was determined finally to impose accountability on a committee that had been in transition. Dan is a strong leader whose word is good and who is basically a decent man. Most of the time, I had very little trouble getting on with him, although he apparently thought I was unnecessarily talkative. He had a very bad time in 1981. Some members beat him on the floor. We beat him with something called the Conable-Hance Bill and he never forgave Kent Hance for that. Kent was a Democratic committee member (and a junior one at that) from Texas. He is now a Republican. Conable-Hance was made up of, or at least half of it was made up of, the old Jones-Conable Bill.

Congressman Jim Jones, an Oklahoman, and a good friend of mine, joined me in proposing depreciation reform legislation in the late 1970s. We had a good run with that effort, and it finally became law, in revised form, in the 1981 Act. In any case, Jimmy Jones and I collaborated on successful legislation, and I do not think Dan has really forgiven Jimmy, either, for that. Dan Rostenkowski believes in loyalty and political teamwork. He remembers when members of his team have tried to build bridges to the other side. Having said that, I want to repeat that Dan Rostenkowski has served as a good leader of the Ways and Means Committee. I don't have any doubt that he will continue to be an effective leader.

PARTISANSHIP AND THE COMMITTEE

Now, in connection with these changes of personnel at the top, there were changes in the Ways and Means Committee as well. I think understanding that is important. Senior Democrats on the committee go back to the days of consensus. They have been strong people, chosen because they had their own following in the House—people like Jake Pickle of Texas, Sam Gibbons of Florida, and Charlie Rangel from Harlem. Generally those who came after them have tended to be people who could be more easily controlled because they were not part of the power structure. There are some sparkling exceptions. There are some very bright, young liberals among the Democrats now on the Ways and Means Committee. Of course, liberals have been voices in the wilderness in Washington in recent years. They are biding their time. However, the strength in that committee is generally at the top, as far as the Democrats are concerned. I haven't dealt with the Republicans yet, but politically, at this point, Republicans on the Ways and Means Committee are hopelessly outnumbered. This is largely because the committee was "stacked" as one of the conditions for Rostenkowski's ascendancy as chairman.

When Al Ullman took over from Wilbur Mills, the party ratio on the committee was changed radically from fifteen Democrats and ten Republicans to twenty-three Democrats and twelve Republicans. This was statistically defensible, although terribly offensive to me and my colleagues, because the party ratio in the House as a whole widened greatly in the post-Watergate era. In the Reagan landslide of 1980, the numbers gap between the parties in the House narrowed sharply, and the committee ratio should have followed suit. It did not, and I complained loudly and bitterly about that, to no avail. Rostenkowski always contended that the Speaker forced him to keep a distorted ratio. I listened, but was never certain about this.

There now are twenty-three Democrats and thirteen Republicans on the committee. If the Democrats are voting as a block, and they usually are, then who cares about the Republicans? The Republicans themselves seem to care, but they do it mostly over in a corner by themselves. The Reagan Republican administration has played to the committee power, generally, and has dealt more with the chairman than its fellow Republicans on the committee.

The Ways and Means Committee thus has changed drastically in the past decade. It has become a subcommittee-structured committee in which accountability is the goal, and if you come from Chicago, you believe in control. Control has been achieved. It is a very effective committee and I suspect it will dominate relations with the Senate over tax matters in future legislation.

That this is so will be largely due to Dan Rostenkowski. He has been single-minded in trying to achieve the kind of control that would permit him to have total accountability to his own party and to his own agendum. He has slowly but surely reduced the authority of the subcommittee chairpersons, thereby enhancing his own position. One of his devices has been the use of staff. When subcommittees were established by Ways and Means, in 1975, subcommittee chairpersons initially had considerable power. They were allowed to assemble their own staffs and could, to some extent, operate independently. But all that changed with Dan Rostenkowski, and, as of now, subcommittee staff leaders are responsible far more to the full committee chairman.

The point is that these Ways and Means committees on which I served (and as indicated, I served on three of them, in effect, with three different chairmen) were substantially different in character. People ask me to compare Rostenkowski and Mills, but there is no comparing them. They operated in completely different political contexts. This human institution changed in such ways and in so many ways that to say "Rosty" is a stronger chairman than Mills would be completely to mislead. Quite simply, they have operated in entirely different frameworks.

Also, as indicated, concurrent with changes in the politics of Ways and Means, concurrent with changes in makeup of its membership and loss of political function by the Democrats, plus imposition of political accountability by the Democratic caucus, there were staff changes of some dimension, too. We had always depended, during Mills' period and for the most part during Ullman's period, on the technical skills of a group called the Joint Committee on Taxation.

This committee provided special technical tax advice both to Ways and Means and to Senate Finance. The Joint Committee did not meet a lot, but it had a highly specialized and skilled staff, headed for many years by a man named Laurence Woodworth, as I mentioned earlier. He was a tax expert, but not a tax lawyer. He did his graduate work in public finance and management, but I think Wilbur Mills and John Byrnes considered him the best tax lawyer they knew. A brilliant man, Woodworth went during the Carter administration to the Treasury Department to be the chief tax policy advisor. I never knew why he did that. It seemed a step down, or at least sideways to me. In any event, he died an untimely death of a stroke shortly after he made the move.

Larry Woodworth was succeeded as Joint Committee chief of staff by Bobby Shapiro and then by Mark McConaghy, two fine tax lawyers, who later went to Price Waterhouse. David Brockway, a specialist in international tax law at one time, next became staff chief, and he was succeeded by Ronald Pearlman, who served as Assistant Treasury Secretary for Tax Policy. Pearlman had been in private practice and Brockway has returned to private practice. I should note that it is *unusual* for someone who has been in private practice to assume command of the joint tax staff. It is *unique* for someone who has been tax policy chief at Treasury to do so. Pearlman followed a route reverse to that taken by Larry Woodworth in the late 1970s.

The joint tax staff served for many years as the Ways and Means Committee's technical arm and the source of our statistics when we were unwilling to accept Treasury statistics, and sometimes we were unwilling. This was very important in the tax-writing process. People who wanted to suggest new clauses in tax laws would not necessarily talk to members first. They would go to the joint tax staff and have them bring up the issue. If the joint tax staff said this or that would not work, the Ways and Means Committee would not pay much attention to it.

The Joint Tax Committee declined in power, however, as tax-writing committees themselves became more politically accountable. It did not decline in expertise—it is still a very expert group. Nevertheless, concurrent with growth of the subcommittee structure and the ascendancy of Dan Rostenkowski, who understood control, the partisan Ways and Means Committee staff achieved an increasing dimension, and the influence of the Joint Committee declined.

Wilbur Mills didn't like a lot of staff around. He wanted members to be part of the total process, except for the expert advice they got from the Joint Committee. That was not the way of Dan Rostenkowski. He not only gained control of the subcommittee staffs, but he built his own central staff, particularly in the tax area. He did this slowly, but within a relatively few years after he became chairman, members found that the committee majority staff was not only greater in numbers, but stronger in specialization. In self-defense, our own Republican staff followed suit, but on a much smaller scale.

Somewhat the same thing was happening in the Senate Finance Committee, where reliance also had been heavily placed on the joint tax staff. When Bob Dole, the very active Senator from Kansas, became chairman in 1981, the Finance Committee's little staff suddenly began to grow, in numbers and in substantive expertise. Inevitably, as these committee staffs—

both Republican and Democratic—assumed larger proportions, usage and the power of the joint tax staff declined commensurately. The partisan staff interposed itself between members and the Joint Committee staff.

By the time I left Ways and Means at the beginning of 1985, there were about seventy-eight majority staffers and eighteen minority staffers, who were required to justify themselves and were gradually taking more and more action away from the Joint Committee. This caused a decline in expertise on the purely technical side. It also meant more political accountability. The Treasury, during the same period of time, also declined in importance in its tax-writing role. Treasury always was the main executive branch department as far as the Ways and Means Committee was concerned. The Secretary of the Treasury frequently appeared in our committee. During periods when we were marking up a bill, especially during the Mills period, the secretary, either Republican or Democrat, would sit at the witness table and participate in the process. Mills, seeking consensus, would want Treasury on board, too.

Following the partisanship of the Nixon period (and that, of course, was everybody's fault), the Treasury got relegated gradually to the seat behind the witness table, then was sent back to the office. Having lost dignity, the secretary no longer came, but sent an agent, and consensus was no longer part of the bridge between the executive and the legislative branches in tax policy.

Procedural changes occurred during this time, too. Common Cause, the citizens' group, had the notion that the average American would leave hearth and home and rush down to see how the government was faring, if he or she could just get into the committee room. We had been having mostly closed meetings up until then. Gradually, the Common Cause campaign for meeting in the "sunshine" became successful and we opened more and more committee meetings to the public—which, of course, hardly ever showed up. Common

Cause was horrified to find that it wasn't the average citizen who rushed down to the room, but the pinstripe-suited lobbyists who came and sat and grimaced as members of the committee failed to act on contracts they thought already had been won from them. The whole environment for decision-making deteriorated.

Of interest to note is that for the major reform bill in 1986, Chairman Rostenkowski closed the markup sessions, and that reflects some general understanding that open markups have not been a total success. One of the problems with open markups is that if very sensitive issues are being considered, this tends to transfer the real situs for decision making to some informal meeting that frequently excludes people who might not agree with decisions being sought. Therefore, there isn't the full base of discussion, compromise, and confrontation desirable in a democratic institution such as the House. Open meetings in recent years also have included conferences between House and Senate on tax matters. Both House and Senate now have to authorize special conference committees explicitly to close their official meetings, and that, of course, is not going to happen.

Senators used to be able to avoid having to discuss substance. If some very distinguished senator had an amendment that was subject to conference decision, senators would simply say to House members: "Well, that's Senator so-and-so's amendment and we just can't talk about it because he isn't here." After awhile, the House might recede without ever having gotten to a discussion of the merits of the issue. When the Conference Committee meets in the open, senators (and House members, for that matter) have to discuss the merits or appear shallow to their public and news media auditors. However, after awhile, the same force—the yearning for privacy—relegates decisions to a private, informal meeting place, with the partisan staff carrying memos, ultimatums, possible deals, et cetera from Ways and Means majority conferees to Senate Finance majority conferees. Public meetings of the Conference Committee frequently are used only to announce decisions arrived at elsewhere.

So, meeting consistently in the "sunshine" has not proved satisfactory for the Committee on Ways and Means. The opening of House-Senate tax conferences has not been an unqualified success, either. Open doors or closed, however, the Ways and Means Committee will continue to do its job in a deliberative way. Even with partisan "stacking," even with a loss of power and some jurisdiction, even with very liberal Democrats in the caucus nipping at its heels, the committee remains essentially conservative (with a lower-case "c"). It will change, of course, when its chairpersons change, but not in its basic purpose and mandate.

CHAPTER 3

THE FEDERAL INCOME TAX:
ONE MAN'S PERSPECTIVE

THERE IS NO ISSUE more central to the relationship between government and people than taxation. This connection was at the very heart of the American Revolution, and its basic dynamics have not changed since then. Today, its Internal Revenue Code is the major device by which the United States government transfers money from the private to the public sector. Most Americans individually have natural resistance to the process, but, collectively, we demand certain services—including national defense—and collectively we pay for these through our tax system.

This process sets the stage for a basic conflict that other countries experience, but which we citizens in the United States seem to have raised to a very high level, indeed. We bombard Washington with demands for special assistance and general largesse, while exerting equally great efforts to minimize our own personal contributions to the common coffer. Exacerbating the problem is the certain knowledge on the part of virtually every taxpayer as to how and where, and to what extent, collected taxes should be spent. These are narrow, albeit often meritorious, views, which managers of government cannot adopt as demanded if they are to do a creditable job of governing in behalf of all.

So the struggle goes on—endlessly—with representatives

of the people squarely in the middle. Members of Congress must be responsive, or at the least must appear to be responsive, to their individual constituents, or they will lose those important votes in the next election. They also must be responsive to generalized demands, and to the need to govern responsibly. They must provide the ways and the means to run the central government, consistent with what people want. The term "ways and means" thus was given (appropriately, I think) to the first standing committee of Congress. Today, the Committee on Ways and Means remains at the center of the process. It has the responsibility to raise whatever revenue the government requires.

Until relatively recently in our national life, this committee turned to other sources than income. From the earliest days of the United States until the Civil War, reliance for revenue rested largely on customs receipts. From 1789 to 1791, customs receipts accounted for about $4.4 million, or more than 99 percent of total governmental income. Nearly one hundred years later, in 1862, total government receipts were about $52 million, with customs intake equaling $49 million, or about 95 percent of total federal revenue. There were other federal taxes between the Revolution and the Civil War, of course. Distilled spirits, sugar, snuff, and legal instruments all were, at one time or another, subject to levy. However, relatively speaking, income produced by these measures was slight.

The Civil War required financing on a much larger scale than allowed by existing income, which gave rise to America's first federal tax on income. Article One (Section 8, clause 1) of the Constitution states:

> The Congress shall have power to lay and collect Taxes, Duties, Imposts and Excises, to pay the Debts and provide for the common Defense and general Welfare of the United States; but all Duties, Imposts and Excises shall be uniform throughout the United States.

Article One (Section 2, clause 3, as well as Article 1, Section

9, clause 4) required that any direct taxes had to be apportioned among the states and had to be based on population distribution.

That first tax on income thus was in two parts: 3 percent on income up to $10,000 and 5 percent on income over $10,000. There was a $600 exemption. Rising war costs led to increased reliance on the income levy and, in 1864, rates rose to 5 percent on income up to $5,000, 7.5 percent on income from $5,000 to $10,000, and 10 percent on income over $10,000. Eventually, these rates reached 5 percent on up to $5,000 of income, and 10 percent on income above $5,000. Public debate was hot, and centered on the question of progressive versus flat rates. Proponents of progressive rates argued that those with greater incomes should pay a disproportionately greater share of government costs, while their opponents leveled charges of inequality, asserting that the rich should not be punished simply because they were rich. The debate abated with repeal of the income levies after the end of the war, but class lines on taxation had formed.

For many years, income taxation was not used federally, but demand for it continued, largely in the West and South, and among farm and labor organizations. Business interests, principally in the East, were aligned in opposition. In 1892, a Populist movement, pushed by labor, farmers, and small business, became a significant political factor. Moreover, one of the Populist Party proposals was a graduated income tax.

After the election of Grover Cleveland to the presidency, adverse economic conditions resulted in a substantial federal revenue deficit, something that appears to have been viewed with much greater apprehension in those days. Complicating matters of that era, President Cleveland was committed to tariff reduction, which meant a further deficit. New revenue sources were required, and the Democratic Party endorsed an income tax. On this issue, in Congress, Democrats from the West and the South faced Republicans, and some other Democrats, of the East. Proponents of the income tax demanded a greater contribution by the wealthy to federal revenues. Opponents mounted a crusade against what they termed a move toward socialism, but agrarian interests of the West and South won the day, and the 1894 income tax was installed. This was levied at 2 percent on individual and corporate net income, with a $4,000 exemption for individuals. Personal property received by gift or inheritance was included in income.

Income tax proponents thus overcame major legislative obstacles, but they still had to clear judicial hurdles. Opponents instituted numerous injunction suits, some in the form of stockholder action to restrain corporations from paying an allegedly unconstitutional tax. The suit that became perhaps most famous was *Pollock v. Farmers' Loan and Trust Company*, decided in 1895. The main constitutional argument of opponents was based on Article One (Sec. 2, clause 3, and Sec. 9, clause 4), requiring apportionment among the states and according to population. Judicial precedents clearly were on the same side of the argument as proponents of the tax, but these precedents were of no avail. The Supreme Court, in a six to two vote, held the income tax unconstitutional on two grounds. First, with regard to income from land, the tax was direct and therefore invalid, because unapportioned. Second, as to income from municipal bonds, the tax was invalid because the federal government lacked authority to impose a tax that falls on the power of the states to borrow money.

The Pollock decision held for eighteen years. However, income tax proponents kept the heat on. In 1908, President Theodore Roosevelt urged a levy on income, and a year later a group of Republican senators—LaFollette, Borah, and others—forced the issue in the Senate by becoming allied with some Democrats who also favored the income levy. Conservative Republicans in Congress, forced to compromise, joined with President Taft and suggested a corporation tax and a constitutional amendment authorizing imposition of an income tax. The compromise succeeded, resulting in passage of the 1909 Corporation Tax of 1 percent on corporate net income over $5,000. This effort also failed in court, being held unconstitutional because it was not deemed a direct tax but an excise tax on business done in the corporate form.

Shortly thereafter, however, the pro-income tax coalition mustered new strength, and Congress formally proposed ratification of the Sixteenth Amendment, which states: "The Congress shall have power to lay and collect taxes on incomes, from whatever source derived, without apportionment among the several States, and without regard to any census or enumeration." Ratification of the amendment was boosted by the election of Woodrow Wilson in 1912, and formal certification that enough states had agreed was made on February 25, 1913.

Democrats and progressive Republicans in Congress, with Wilson's backing, then passed the 1913 Income Tax. It provided for a "normal" tax of 1 percent on individual net incomes, with a $3,000 exemption, plus an additional $1,000 exemption for married persons. There was a graduated "surtax" of 1 percent to 6 percent on income above $20,000. Corporate net income was subject to a 1 percent tax. Opponents of income taxation again took their case to the courts, relying largely on alleged violation of the uniformity clause, because of various exemptions and classifications. The Supreme Court brushed these objections aside, however, and in *Brushaber v. Union Pacific Railroad Company* (1916), upheld the tax, and relegated the *Pollock* case decision to the position of an historical footnote. A second income tax bill became law in 1916. This one also provided for an estate tax. A gift tax was added in 1924, repealed in 1926, and reinstated in 1932.

The new income tax became the chief revenue raiser during World War I, when governmental spending understandably soared. In the Revenue Act of 1918, rates were 6 percent on the first $4,000 of income and 12 percent on the balance. Atop that was a surtax, starting at 1 percent on income above $5,000 and graduated to 65 percent on income of $1 million. Exemptions were $1,000 for singles, $2,000 for married persons, and

$200 for each dependent. The corporate rate was 12 percent, with a $2,000 exemption. An excess profits tax also was imposed. Because of exemption levels, relatively high for the times, only a small percentage of people paid any income taxes. There were, in 1920, about 5.5 million individual income tax returns, from a population of some 106 million. The income tax thus was, in its early years, a levy essentially on more well-to-do Americans.

In the 1920s, a general prosperity brought about lowered rates, but no repeal. Income tax was becoming entrenched as this country's largest single source of revenue. Its scope and complexity grew steadily. In the Revenue Act of 1928, its provisions were rearranged completely into a form, and numbering of sections, which existed, with a few adjustments, until the wholesale revamping of the structure in 1954.

With the Great Depression, rates turned up again and exemptions dropped. In 1932, a federal sales tax was proposed and enjoyed some months in the sun of public debate before fading into obscurity. In the wake of this debate, a number of federal excise taxes did succeed, and soon became an equally prolific source of revenue up until World War II. Also, with the advent of the New Deal, rates were increased on upper-bracket taxpayers, and by 1938 the normal tax was 4 percent, while the surtax rose from 4 percent to 75 percent on incomes up to $5 million. Exemptions were: $1,000 for a single person, $2,500 for a married person, and $400 per dependent. A family of four with an income of $10,000 was paying about $340 a year in income taxes.

Financial pressures of World War II resulted in broad-based reforms. Exemption for singles was dropped to $500. A surtax was applied on the first dollar of taxable income. For those at the $14,000 income bracket, a combined rate of 50 percent was applied. By 1945, about 43 million persons were filing taxable returns. A family earning $10,000 was paying more than $2,000 a year. Corporations were tapped more heavily. The top corporate rate rose from 19 percent in 1938 to 40 percent in 1945, and an excess profits rate of 89.5 percent was imposed, with the result that the overall maximum rate on corporations reached 80 percent.

World War II also brought on the present system of withholding, solving a growing problem of non-compliance as rates soared and the tax base sprawled. A bureaucrat named Beardsley Ruml rose from obscurity to instant fame—or perhaps more accurately to notoriety—by advocating, and thus becoming the father of, the pay-as-you-go system of income taxation. Several simple (simple by hindsight) tax forms were devised. One called for an employee to state his or her wages, attach withholding receipts, and send in the little package to the Bureau of Internal Revenue. Another form enabled a taxpayer to compute taxes that were owed by using, for the first time, a table, which originally required only two pieces of information: gross income and exemptions. The table and the withholding system were backed up by a new standard deduction equal to 10 percent of gross income (this in lieu of itemizing separate deductions) and an across-the-board exemption of $500 per taxpayer and dependent.

The withholding development changed perceptions about our income tax structure more than any other change since the first income tax—at least for a while. When people had to save their money so they could meet their tax obligations, all at once, after the first of the year, outrage at the size of the tax, and the visibility of government's demands (not to mention non-payment by the uninformed) imposed some real restraint on legislators. Once the process became almost automatic for wage-earners through withholding, tax filings soared. Overwithholding encouraged compliance, in the interest of refunds, and some even used the system as an opportunity for forced savings, to be achieved through refunds.

The Korean War led to another series of tax rate increases. There was an introduction of the split-income method of taxing married couples. A third taxpayer category was added—the head of household. Liability in this designation was placed halfway between that of a married couple filing a joint return and that of a single taxpayer.

In 1952, President Eisenhower was elected and carried with him enough candidates to put both houses of Congress under Republican control—perhaps for the last time. Although Republicans gained majority status in the Senate with the Reagan "sweep" in 1980, Republicans have not constituted a full congressional majority since 1954. In that year, individual rates came down. The $10,000-income family was paying about $1,500 by then. Corporate rates were scheduled for reduction, and most excise levies were cut by 50 percent. Also that year, the entire Internal Revenue Code was revised. Most provisions were rearranged, terminology was standardized, normal and surtaxes were merged, and the Bureau of Internal Revenue was changed in name to the Internal Revenue Service.

However, truly substantial and significant changes in the 1954 Code were in policy. There was a greater stress on tax incentives to investment, as evidenced by a more rapid write-off of depreciation allowances on new assets. There were also reductions in tax for persons aged sixty-five and older who were receiving pensions and unearned income. Also, new deductions for child-care expenses were allowed. Revised treatments of partnerships, estates and trusts, annuities, and corporate distributions increased tax complexity.

EQUITY AND COMPLEXITY

At this point, consideration of specific forces at work in the legislative environment of the income tax improves understanding of how the Internal Revenue Code is still developing. First, as the income tax system became more complex, something that might be called the ABC syndrome developed. With the birth of the brand new Internal Revenue Code of 1954, this phenomenon burst into full bloom. Here is basically how the syndrome works. Suppose that someone—a business person, a wage earner, or a retired person—approaches his or her representative in Congress and says, in effect: "What you have done in the tax system is fundamentally all right, but I have a very unusual situation, you see, and it is not fair for me to have to be taxed this way just because my neighbor thinks it is all right." Suppose further that the member of Congress looks at the matter and agrees with the taxpayer, called "A." The member takes the case to the Committee on Ways and Means, and the committee also finds that "A" is, indeed, in a different situation and should be treated differently, i.e., more fairly. So, "A" gets an exception in the tax code—an exception that fits all other "A's" who are similarly situated. A year or so passes and along comes taxpayer "B," who tells Congress: "What you did for 'A' was good. It is an appropriate exception. But I am situated a little differently and what you did for 'A' is having an adverse effect on me. Please take a look and see if you don't agree." Of course, Congress does agree, and provides an exception to the exception in order to take care of "B." Then, about a year later, taxpayer "C" approaches Congress, and you know what happens. An exception to the exception to the exception for "C."

Congress wasn't trying to complicate the process. It was simply trying to be responsive to a tremendous diversity in sources of income and different circumstances of taxpayers. A relatively few years of this sort of thing finally achieved a cumbersome code. This code reflected, to a rather high degree, the desire of Congress to respond to taxpayer sensitivity, a need for equity in democratic tax issues, and tremendous diversity in our free enterprise economy. Obviously, not all changes made in the Internal Revenue Code over the years resulted from the ABC chain reaction. However, many did. Many other types of alterations were driven by comparable wants and needs, real, or as perceived by sensitive political antenna.

In a collective—in the PTA back home, for example—compromise is sometimes necessary about such simple things as the date for the annual school picnic. So it is with the Committee on Ways and Means and tax legislation. Compromise brings complexity because it tries to make everybody happy. Compromise is not necessarily related to equity so much as to the need to get majority support where a variety of interests are involved. Thus compromise, normal for legislators, is inevitably the enemy of both consistency and simplicity.

What have been the characteristics of typical tax bills of the past? First, they have normally been responses to outside influence, rarely to congressional initiative. Sometimes the legislative staff would bring forward some idea or concept. Sometimes an individual congressman would be outraged by something in a Jack Anderson column about a loophole scandal of one sort or another. Generally, however, big tax bills came as a result of pressure from the executive branch of our federal government, which had to administer complicated tax laws through the internal revenue system. In our crisis-motivated system, sensitivity of the subject matter of taxation has easily created crises—with the same regularity as elections. Fluid responses by the tax-sensitive to tax incentives have constantly brought unexpected results. Action on tax revision was rarely something generated within the tax-writing committees themselves. They always have tended to grind away on routine legislation for the most part until some gathering storm required a response.

Next, the typical tax bill of the past fostered a gradual growth of preferences. This resulted in a consequent narrowing of the base, and a resulting increase in progressivity of tax rates on what remained subject to taxation. What is a tax preference? It is simply deferral or exclusion from taxation of some part of, some element of, economic income. It could be a deduction or a credit, possibly an exemption. Normally, American tax writers have dealt with changes in the tax law through creation of new preferences, and not through changes in the rate of tax. The result of repetitive tax reforms, then, was to load the system down with preferences.

A third characteristic of the typical tax bill of the past was that it "bought" reform. If the average American developed a suspicion that he or she was paying too much tax because somebody else was not paying enough, then those in Congress knew that no legislation would be generally accepted as tax reform unless average Americans could get to the bottom line and see their taxes going down. If they saw that happening, they would say, "Ah. That is indeed real reform." In their view (and politicians willingly confirmed this) they had been paying too much tax because others hadn't been paying enough. If their payments didn't go down, tax change wasn't reform, but fraud. So, Congress "bought" tax reform through rate cuts concurrent with requested structural changes. This was possible because of bracket creep.

In any event, Congress did not change laws just to complicate people's lives, or to confuse their thinking, or to make them unhappy. Most of the time Congress has changed tax laws because of members' understandable and predictable desires to respond to people—to confer a benefit (or a perceived benefit) on some sensitive group of taxpayers. Legislators generally want to respond affirmatively and positively to what is seen as diversity, and sometimes inequity, among millions of taxpayers who want or need a little adjustment.

However, as more and more adjustments, or exceptions, were enacted, more and more income was no longer subject to tax. This meant that, to raise the same amount of revenue the economic income remaining subject to tax had to be taxed a little more steeply. In short, there was a narrowing tax base and an increasingly progressive system, which went on for years.

BRACKET CREEP

Now, let's further define the phenomenon called "bracket creep." Brackets were an inherent part of the progressive system in which graduated rates were applied to bracketed income. The higher the bracket, the higher the rate. What could be fairer than taxing the affluent more on gains made that ex-

ceeded a reasonable cost of living? Inflation grew rapidly over
these years, and as workers were given "cost-of-living" increases in wages and salaries to help them keep up with inflation, their income gradually moved up, from one bracket to
the next, and was taxed at higher and higher rates. Hence the
term, "bracket creep." Taxpayers were paid more money, but
it was worth less, and they were paying progressively more
taxes on it. They were taxed on nominal, not real, income.
They were on a taxation treadmill.

The federal government was the prime beneficiary of
bracket creep. All Congress had to do was continue existing
policy and collect increasing revenue, automatically. Government spending could be increased without tax rates rising.
This "fiscal dividend" was a politician's delight. Taxes did not
have to be raised through overt political action. More money
came in automatically, thanks to inflation, to pay for more
government services or occasional tax cuts, depending on
where the popular pressure was most intense. During the in-
flationary 1970s, as much as $30-to-$60 billion a year extra
flowed into the Treasury through bracket creep. Growth in
government was paid for automatically; the deficit did not go
up. Congress was able to provide modest tax cuts selectively
during that period, while the total tax burden increased.

This was, generally, the pattern of tax revision through
the late 1960s and all of the 1970s. I worked on seven major
reform measures—and many more of somewhat lesser importance—during most of this period as a member of the
Committee on Ways and Means. We made tax changes that
were, for the most part, modestly redistributive. We did that
because as people marched through brackets, obviously more
and more poorer people were destined to get on the tax rolls.
Adjustment of the law was necessary so they wouldn't go on
the tax rolls if they were simply getting more little pieces of
green paper worth less and less. So, the system tended to become more redistributive to take care particularly of people at
the bottom end of the tax scale. There was enough regressive

taxation around (excise, sales, real estate, etc.) to increase their burdens, without adding bracket creep in the progressive income tax to their problems.

There was difficulty doing much for those at the top of the income scale who were already at the maximum tax level. Obviously, their taxes were not going to be cut generally. The result was that the middle class tended to move up toward the top, while the top rate stayed unchanged, at whatever the maximum was. The trend, then, of tax bills over the past twenty years was gradually to put more burden on the middle class, and to drop the lower income groups entirely off the tax rolls. As I noted, that is one of the reasons for the traditional distribution pattern of the 1970s. But all this changed in the 1981 tax act. It was not typical of the pattern, but I am going to address that separately, a bit later.

THE 1969 ACT

The first big tax bill I experienced as a Ways and Means Committee member (and I should note that I was a very junior member at that time) was the 1969 Tax Reform Act. This was easily the most far-reaching revision of the Code since 1954, and arose in large part from publicly-voiced concern that too many well-to-do Americans were entirely avoiding taxation. Joseph Barr, who was Secretary of the Treasury for a short period of time during the waning days of the Lyndon Johnson administration, announced that more than two hundred millionaires were paying no income tax, for one reason or another. This revelation hit the Ways and Means Committee like the proverbial bombshell. Collectively, we went into a figurative state of shock, as I recall and—being a responsive group—started almost immediately preparing a tax reform bill. Needless to say, we were outraged because the public was outraged.

For many of my colleagues, the aim throughout was to decrease the possibility that wealthy taxpayers could avoid paying a respectable share of total collected taxes. In the process, a number of so-called loopholes were closed. As I noted in House debate on the bill, ". . . there is no question that one man's loophole is another man's needed national priority." Through our tax laws are expressed our sense of national priorities. Things identified as loopholes were not originally put in the law to make the rich richer, but to help channel the flow of funds into areas of national need. Normally, tax preference, which becomes identified popularly as a loophole, can be closed only at a cost to the nation. Congress, representing the people, must assess the cost and determine if it is worth the closure.

The 1969 Act closed many of these loopholes in a selectively responsible way. I was, in fact, proud to be part of that process. I thought we closed most, if not all, those loopholes identified at the time as scandalous, and we limited many preferences that were of questionable national value. The 1969 Act also dealt with the uproar caused by Secretary Barr's disclosures in a way that greatly complicated the law for people with large tax preferences, by adding the "minimum tax" concept. If individual tax preference is an incentive to socially valuable investment, too much preference in individual cases would result in the wealthy not paying as much tax as others thought they should. So, Congress started taxing well-to-do people not just on their taxable income, but also on their aggregate tax preferences, if these were large in proportion to what they would otherwise owe. Thus was woven a complicated net to catch big fish that, for one reason or another, might get away, to the outrage of smaller fish.

THE 1971 ACT

The Revenue Act of 1971 was important, too. Essentially, it was a classic example of the way laws are made; that is, the president proposes and Congress disposes. President Nixon, reacting to an economic downturn, proposed legislation to cut individual taxes and to stimulate business expansion. The bill that was proposed was fine-tuned by the Committee on

Ways and Means and expeditiously moved to passage and finally to enactment. It reinstituted the old Investment Tax Credit (ITC) at 7 percent. The ITC had been adopted in the 1960s, then repealed. When business became sluggish, back came the ITC. Changing it will always be a congressional temptation to fire up incentives for investment in capital goods when times are bad, or, if times are good, to reduce "giveaways" to business. This preference, because it seems to work, gets manipulated more than most. The 1971 bill also provided for a new and more rapid write-off of industrial machinery and equipment called the Asset Depreciation Range (ADR) and for a new set of provisions to promote exports through a Domestic International Sales Corporation (DISC), which would provide certain tax benefits through foreign sales, thus encouraging production at home for export rather than production abroad through foreign subsidiaries of domestic corporations.

THE 1976 ACT

The third major tax revision to come along while I served on Ways and Means was the 1976 Tax Reform Act. I was, as I recall, less enthusiastic about this measure because when it was debated in the House it included a substantial tax cut without any linkage to a limitation on expenditures. I thought then, considering the state of the economy, the two had to be connected. Congress was more sensitive to deficits in those days. The central idea behind the 1976 bill was to clamp down on tax shelters. One of the problems I had was with a decision by the conferees to limit deductions to amounts for which an investor was "at risk" in a particular activity. I thought there was too broad a reliance on the "at risk" test. I also thought there was too much reliance on beefing up the minimum tax, especially with respect to long-term capital gains. I wanted to see those rates reduced. They were not. By increasing the minimum rate from 10 to 15 percent, the 1976 legislation was, in effect, destined to boost the effective rate on capital gains.

Studies showed that about 85 percent of the revenue from individual minimum tax came from previously untaxed portions of long-term gains.

The conferees also extended the 10 percent investment tax credit to the end of 1980. I was not a leading advocate of the investment tax credit approach, preferring realistic depreciation schedules and allowances. What concerned me most about the conferees' actions in this area, however, was a provision to permit a total investment credit as high as 11.5 percent if the employer established a qualified Employee Stock Ownership Plan (ESOP). I believed that was essentially a gimmicky approach, which Congress would be well-advised to restrain. I was particularly concerned about the damage that growth of these ESOP plans might do to well-established and more traditional profit-sharing and pensions plans, upon which so many American workers have relied.

With regard to Domestic International Sales Corporations (DISCs), conferees attempted to compromise competing needs and philosophies. I strongly supported the DISC concept and believed the conference compromise to be less than desirable, but nonetheless workable. It retained the major portion of DISC benefits and the incentive for creation of American jobs resulting from those benefits, while at the same time reducing revenue loss. Essentially, the conference agreement provided for continued DISC benefits to the extent that current gross export receipts exceeded two-thirds of a DISC's gross receipts in a four-year base period.

In addition, the conferees agreed to real property valuation provisions regarding certain property devoted to farming or other closely-held businesses, extending the time for payment of estate tax liabilities in such cases, and restricting "generation skipping" transfers made free of estate taxation. Overall, I think these provisions constituted a desirable change in the law. Despite problems I had with specifics of the legislation, I consistently supported it as a whole. It represented a modest reform effort, but modesty is not always bad, and it was not bad then. There was a general move toward greater equity, and I always have been in favor of that.

THE 1978 ACT

The 1978 Tax Act was, in many respects, a more exciting venture. I'm going to dwell on this interesting proposal at some length as an illustration of the by-play that goes on during tax legislation. Carter was in his second year as president, and was beginning to talk about his plans for a major tax bill. Nothing definitive emerged for some time, however, and I gleaned much of the information I had about it from Mike Blumenthal, the new Secretary of the Treasury. He called on me in my office several times, talking in generalizations at first, and probing for an understanding of the Ways and Means Committee and other institutions in which I served in Congress. He was somewhat aloof and ascetic, but thoughtful and very sincere in his effort to do a good job and reflect credit on the administration.

During these talks, I not only learned a bit about what was important to the administration in terms of tax policy, but I got a glimpse of the inner workings of the Carter presidency. I recall thinking at the time that if the president were not so bright, if he were not a speed reader, and if he were not willing to work from 5:30 in the morning until after midnight every day, he might have realized more quickly that one cannot conduct the presidency alone. His very virtues were prolonging his isolation. Further, and this seemed especially appropriate with respect to tax policy, he showed no signs of interest in persuading instead of judging.

Secretary Blumenthal eventually indicated that he and other administration officials were reviewing tax policy and that legislation was likely. When the Carter tax plan finally emerged—after four rewrites, I was told—it had a centerpiece that called for a total reduction in revenues of $25 billion, on a one-time basis. The Committee on Ways and Means took up the proposal in late spring with the usual amount of "hoopla" that accompanies a presidential tax initiative, and set about the traditional and laborious process of working its own collective will on the chief executive's legislation. Amendments were considered and some were adopted, including one I brought forward along with a Democratic colleague, Joe Fisher, an economist and relatively new member who represented a Northern Virginia constituency.

What we proposed came to be known as the "above-the-line" charitable deduction, allowing taxpayers who did not itemize also to be able to claim a deduction based on their contributions to charity. President Carter wanted to cut taxes in large part by increasing the standard deduction, on the theory that poor people usually did not itemize. This reduced the number of people with incentives to give to charity, which Fisher and I found unfortunate. One result, as some of us saw it, was that the base of philanthropy in the country was being narrowed, damaging pluralism in our society. If many fewer people could claim them, we feared that charitable deductions would begin to look like loopholes rather than justified preferences. Our amendment was accepted by the committee without much disagreement, even though the administration strongly opposed it, on the main ground that it did not simplify the tax code—an announced primary goal of the president's package.

However, the most contentious issue was elsewhere. Rather early in the committee markup, I began to hear conversation about a proposal offered by my Republican colleague, the late Bill Steiger of Wisconsin. Bill was one of the brightest members in Congress, often serving as a catalyst, bringing about workable compromises between opposing committee forces. He had come up with the notion that a rollback of the effective tax rate on capital gains would serve as an economic stimulant, and would also be popular. An informal poll taken by the chairman showed that twenty-seven of the thirty-seven committee members would support it. President Carter, however, strongly opposed any reduction of the capital gains rate as benefitting the rich, whether or not it would benefit the economy.

While discussion of the Steiger amendment was going on, Chairman Al Ullman suspended committee deliberations until, as he explained it, a comprehensive tax package, with clear support of the committee majority as well as the administration, could be developed. Privately, he expressed concern that if the Steiger amendment to the president's bill were adopted, a substitute by our colleague, Charles Vanik of Ohio, would be offered and accepted. The Vanik amendment would have scuttled just about everything in the package except a one-time tax cut of $9 billion. A number of liberals had indicated they would jump at the chance to vote for such a proposal, and Ullman feared that it might be passed by the House and that the Senate would then adopt a serious, major tax-reform measure. If that happened, Al and I knew we would have to go to conference without a House position on anything except the temporary tax reduction. We would be trapped and probably forced to accept much of a Senate bill that could be unappealing to the House.

Behind this explanation of the suspension, however, was the strong and obvious opposition of the administration to the Steiger amendment, and Al Ullman's uncertainty about how to deal further with a popular and Republican-backed plan under those conditions. The suspension continued for weeks. After about a month, Mike Blumenthal came to see me and said that Al Ullman had told him I refused to compromise on the Steiger amendment. I explained that this was not the case, and suggested that if Mike were serious about compromising, he should deal directly with Steiger. I then called Steiger, told him of my conversation with Mike, and suggested the two get together.

Before any progress could take place on that front, Steiger was approached by Jim Jones of Oklahoma, a mutual friend who said he had license from Ullman to work on his own compromise apart from the administration's efforts. Jones wanted not only to cut back on the capital gains tax but to grant some relief to taxpayers with incomes between $15,000 and $50,000. Secretary Blumenthal then reentered the picture, flanked this time by Charles Schultze, the chairman of the Council of Economic Advisors, and Stu Eisenstadt, the president's domestic policy advisor. They condemned both the Steiger amendment and the Jones compromise as awful alternatives and threatened a veto if either reached the president's desk. Despite their intense lobbying, I got the impression they held the Steiger-Jones package in low esteem largely because the president held it in low esteem.

Whatever the reason, Ullman took them seriously, and again backed off the entire exercise. He told me at the time: "Barber, you and I know they're not going to get anything better than the Jones package, and I have told the secretary that if he has not accomplished anything within two weeks, I will resume control and we will pass the Jones package in the Committee." During that hiatus, I remember thinking that I could not recall a period in my service in the Ways and Means Committee when we had done so little work and been so frustrated. The entire Carter program had been before the committee for months and nothing had really happened to move it along or to jettison it in favor of something else. Eventually, of course, the committee did resume its deliberations, and things moved along reasonably rapidly after that. Only a relatively few amendments were adopted. Not among them was the Fisher-Conable plan for above-the-line charitable contributions. It was a good issue and it remained alive. I believed—correctly, as events turned out—that it would fare better at another time in another context.

The committee passed the tax bill, handily, with the Jones compromise, plus a version of the president's temporary tax reduction. Al Ullman felt he had been realistic, although he had bucked the president, the House Democratic leadership, the Treasury Department, and a liberal majority. He felt, quite rightly, that his leadership ability had been demonstrated and his prestige enhanced. The Senate soon developed its own bill, a conference was held, and the resulting legislation retained the basic ingredients passed by the House. In the process, the president began making noises to the effect that he really had not been opposed to the basic idea of rolling back the capital gains tax, but to the method employed. I recall telling people that the president seemed to be constantly painting himself into a corner, then having to walk through the wet paint, leaving embarrassing tracks in his wake. Although the president "sat" on the completed measure for days, he ultimately signed it—quietly and out of sight—at Camp David.

The final product was not redistributional. It did not take from one group, by taxing them more heavily, in order to give to others. At that time, 60 percent of all federal income taxes collected were paid by only 16 percent of all those subject to tax. The 1978 bill cut taxes, but it spread its relief across various society sectors in the same proportion by which each bore the tax burden. I did not, at the time, believe the overall tax reduction was adequate, but I did applaud the fairness with which modest cuts were distributed.

THE ECONOMIC RECOVERY TAX ACT

The final three major tax reforms with which I dealt, firsthand, came during President Ronald Reagan's first term. The first of these reform measures was, in several respects, the greatest in terms of its lasting impact on tax policy and economic policy. It was an effort with which I was closely associated, both by name and professional interest. The legislation eventually became known as the Economic Recovery Tax Act (ERTA). It evolved at a time when public discussion was focused on many major policy changes, two of which had developed strong followings in the early days of the Reagan administration. One was a proposal for more rapid write-offs of machinery, equipment, and structures; the other called for a sharp reduction in individual income taxes.

For a long time, I had been convinced that the Asset Depreciation Range (ADR) adopted in the 1971 Revenue Act had become outmoded. The nation's economy was in real need of a lift, on a long-term basis, and I worked with Jim Jones, my friend and colleague from Oklahoma, on a new plan, popularly referred to as "10–5–3" because it provided for writing off buildings in ten years, machinery and equipment in five, and automobiles in three. Although it had not gotten even close to enactment, the Jones-Conable bill did get a great deal of favorable attention. Jones and I, both essentially advocates of liberal trade policies, saw depreciation reform as improving industrial competitiveness by encouraging more investment in capital goods rather than reducing corporate taxes in ways that would increase profitability.

Also getting a lot of publicity was a proposal by Jack Kemp, the Republican congressman who represented a neighboring upstate New York district centered in Buffalo, and Bill Roth, the Republican Senator from Delaware. Kemp-Roth, as this plan was dubbed, would cut individual income tax rates by 30 percent across-the-board over three years. It became the centerpiece of the president's own tax plan. Further available for public scrutiny were the outlines of a bill being developed by Dan Rostenkowski. At a press briefing in March of 1981, he announced some of the items he planned to bring before the committee. Among them were a softening of the so-called marriage penalty (then current law had a particularly harmful effect on couples with two substantial incomes), a reduction in the long-term capital gains rate, and a reduction of maximum individual income tax rate from 70 to 50 percent. These constituted Dan's competitive responses to the Reagan program, designed to appeal to conservatives, especially those serving with me on Ways and Means.

Shortly after the Rostenkowski announcement, I was called to the White House to talk with the president about tax strategy. I was told in advance that some of his advisers wanted an alternative to a pure Kemp-Roth proposal, but that President

Reagan was adamant in support of broad tax cuts without embellishment. At the meeting, the president confirmed that he was, indeed, committed to Kemp-Roth, and that he expected Ways and Means Republicans to stick with him on that. I said I could do so cheerfully, but I did not know if all of my colleagues would follow, pointing out that they—as well as I—really liked some provisions that Rostenkowski had talked about. I also told him the Kemp-Roth bill stood little chance in the committee, because of the partisan ratio—twenty-three Democrats to only twelve Republicans. In no uncertain terms, the president replied that he expected us to go down fighting in defense of Kemp-Roth and instructed me not to participate in any compromise.

When I left the meeting, I recall thinking that Reagan appeared in complete charge, that his staff seemed far from anxious to tangle with him (at least on that one issue), and that they preferred to have someone like a sacrificial and expendable Conable come down and give the president the bad news when it appeared he might not have his way with the Ways and Means Committee. Nothing electrifying happened with respect to taxation after that meeting, and there matters stood while the House began dealing with the budget. A budget resolution had to be passed that spring, and David Stockman, mercurial director of the Office of Management and Budget, had been plotting with both House Republicans on the Budget Committee and with conservative Democrats, to form an alternative to the bill being developed by the Democratic majority. Their product was named for Delbert Latta, ranking Republican on the committee, and Phil Gramm, a slow-talking but fast-thinking Texas Democrat who was an integral part of the Stockman conspiracy.

Taking note of the budget action is important, in order to understand more fully the sequence of events leading to the tax bill that followed. The second event would have been considerably different if the budget issue had not been resolved as it was. For example, if budget efforts by Stockman and company had failed, impetus for a radical tax cut would not have had the same political momentum that carried it to enactment.

When the Rules Committee, which is an arm of the House leadership, refused to grant a rule governing debate that would allow a straight up or down vote on the Gramm-Latta alternative, we Republicans became energized. With cooperation from the White House, a counterattack was organized, and the support of all conservative Democrats was solicited. A vote on the rule was scheduled to come up at 11 A.M. the next day. To buy time for some last-minute lobbying, especially of dissident Democrats, House Republican leaders organized a prolonged series of one-minute speeches, which are routinely permitted prior to the start of regularly scheduled legislative business. This tactic postponed the vote until about 1:00 P.M., and by then the tension in the House chamber was palpable. As the voting was reported on electronic "scoreboards" at either end of the chamber, members watched with mounting interest. When both the "yeas" and "nays" passed the two-hundred mark, all eyes were focused intently on the tally board. The final result, 217 against the rule and 210 in favor of it, was greeted by wild cheering on the Republican side of the room and both anguished and angry looks on the other side.

The vote allowed the Gramm-Latta alternative to come up under a new rule. However, when the bill arrived the next morning, it was in great disarray, much of it garbled. After loud complaining of irregularities by Democrats and an equally loud defense from us Republicans, discovery was made that the legislation had been tampered with overnight by elements of the Democratic Study Group, reportedly led by Phil Burton, the San Francisco Democrat (now deceased) who had been defeated by one vote in a contest with Jim Wright for the Majority Leader's post. That discovery subdued the Democrats to some extent and certainly eased any embarrassment on the part of Republicans. I was so enraged that when my turn to speak in behalf of the alternative came, I arose and delivered a speech that was not very coherent, but must have been suitably defiant because it received a rousing response from my side of the aisle. I used the moment to vent some of my long-standing resentment at the "stacking" of Ways and Means against the minority. I also noted in the process that the vote on the rule had proved that an arrogant majority's flexing its muscle on the floor was harder, where the party ratio was about five to four, than in our committee, where the ratio was wider than two to one. The final vote, on the Republican substitute, was favorable, although narrowly so. As far as I was concerned, the joy of victory was short-lived, because I was already beginning to worry about the next confrontation on taxes.

Soon after the budget vote, there was some public discussion—led by Bob Novak, the newspaper columnist—about using a comparable political strategy on the administration's tax bill. This was merging the Kemp-Roth concept with the old Jones-Conable accelerated depreciation bill and having the combination co-sponsored by me and by Kent Hance, a young Texas Democrat in his first term on the Ways and Means Committee. The White House liked the prospect of once more drawing winning support from both mainstream Republicans and conservative Democrats. Eventually, I agreed to the linkage, and was invited to the White House for a strategy session a day before the announcement of the new legislation. Just as I had feared, but expected, I was told that the measure would be decorated with a number of additions, including preferences favoring oil interests, to keep southwestern Democrats on board.

The additions were to be paid for by cutting back on the Jones-Conable part of the package, and you can imagine how pleased I was at this revelation. The write-off period for depreciable real estate was moved from ten years to fifteen years and the 200 percent declining balance was reduced to 150 percent. Despite my unhappiness, the White House strategy worked. Reagan's people knew that most Republicans ultimately would accept an altered package because of loyalty to party and a strong president, and that many conservative Democrats would agree to the deal because they had been given substantial concessions.

While all this was going on, the Finance Committee, under Chairman Bob Dole, had been formulating a bill that followed generally, but with some deviations, the administration's grand plan. Dan Rostenkowski at that point appeared to be committed to a bill that would appeal primarily to his party's liberal majority, which was, essentially, a "loophole" closer. Within days, the administration began to revise Hance-Conable even further, to keep some complaining backers on board and to attract other members who indicated they might get on the bandwagon if the price were right. I talked with Kent Hance about the alterations, and suggested that he not take too much specific pride in authorship because changes were on the way. Hance was visibly upset to learn that I anticipated a Hance-Conable II, but I explained that the administration game plan made sense, in that a successful package more closely attuned to legislation the Senate was formulating would cut down on differences to be reconciled in conference. I probably sounded confident and experienced, because Hance appeared mollified, but underneath my words was a burning frustration at having so little management control over a bill bearing my name, and having so few committee votes at hand to effect a final outcome. However, as I had told the president on more than one occasion, I would help him whenever I could, not only because I agreed with the thrust of what he was trying to achieve, but because our beleaguered minority on an unfairly-stacked committee had to rely on his strength in order to have any clout at all.

Conable-Hance, as the Republicans were calling the measure, was continuing to gain acceptance, but Dan Rostenkowski, seeing how the wind was blowing, modified his original bill in ways that threatened to give the Democrats an edge in the drive for votes. In his usual, careful manner, he had his staff draft additions that were designed to attract a variety of special interests. He asked, and was given, a pledge of support for each adjustment to his package. Conceding the popularity of the president's tax-cutting program, the new Rostenkowski bill included first a one-year rate reduction, then a two-year reduction, with a trigger mechanism allowing a third-year cut.

In a very real sense, a bidding war had broken out, as both sides made changes in response to clamors for more and more "goodies" by would-be supporters. Just before floor debate was to begin, the Conable-Hance strategy team met at the White House to negotiate a final product, which, in an effort to outdo Rostenkowski, seemed to offer nearly everything that anyone's heart might desire. In the bidding process, I fought for indexing of marginal rates. I was convinced then, as I am now, that tying the rates to cost-of-living advances and thus killing bracket creep well might be the most important tax policy change in modern times. Without indexing, Kemp-Roth cuts would soon be offset by bracket creep. Indexing the brackets (raising them each year by an amount comparable to the rise in the cost of living) had an honest logic to it that appealed to me. With indexing, taxes wouldn't go up every year as inflation pushed taxpayers into higher nominal brackets. Thereafter, if Congress wanted to raise taxes, this would have to be part of the law rather than the result of inflation.

Cowards hated the indexing concept, as did budget people like Dave Stockman, who correctly assumed Congress wouldn't have the guts to raise taxes just to keep the deficit down. As a tax measure, though, I thought indexing was more important to an honest tax system than any ephemeral benefit to be gained by an isolated tax cut, even of the Kemp-

Roth dimension. As it turned out, a declining rate of inflation during the 1980s reduced the impact I thought indexing would have. In principle, it's still good, even though it has had a negative impact on the revenue side of the budget. I continue to think Congress should raise taxes explicitly when necessary, rather than rely on inflation to push people into higher brackets. At any rate, I prevailed in White House arguments about this issue when the bill was being put in final form.

Despite that personal victory, I was not optimistic that we could carry the day on the floor. Kent Hance said he could not assure us of more than fifteen Democratic votes, and I could not guarantee that as many as ten Republicans would not cross over, attracted by Rostenkowski's competitive bids to conservatives. However, the president and his staff waged a formidable lobbying campaign, and the Rules Committee obligingly gave us, without a fight, the right to offer our substitute for a straight, up or down, vote. Two days before the debate was scheduled, I began to believe we really had a chance. The next day, head counts showed we probably would win. The final vote was almost anticlimactic. We won by a surprising margin, 238 to 195, with 48 Democrats crossing over. The result was a personal triumph for the president. Chairman Rostenkowski was crushed, and vowed not to be beaten again. He never has been.

Inasmuch as the Senate already had passed its own bill by then, we moved quickly to conference. The leaders of the two committees knew how to bring a conference to a speedy conclusion. It began at 4 P.M. on a Friday and continued virtually non-stop until 8 A.M. the next day. From the House side, there were five Democrats and three Republicans. The Senate sent four Republicans and three Democrats. Rostenkowski was chairman of the conference, and called us to order in H–208, a small room in the Capitol reserved for the chairman of our committee, just off the House floor. There was space enough only for the conferees, a few staffers, a very few re-

porters, (the press usually "pooled" its coverage) and for virtually none of the importunate and disorderly lobbyists who
clustered in the hallway outside, laying hands on the person
of any conferee unlucky enough to have to leave occasionally.

Room H–208 had been used effectively by Ways and Means
chairmen through the years. It had little breathing space in
any event, and with the heat turned up, and cigars lit, pressure often mounted very rapidly to conclude a session and
get outside. On this occasion, cigars were discouraged, but it
was overly warm, and desires to abandon the room became
stronger with each passing hour. Throughout the night we
worked our way past a hundred or so items on which the Senate and House bills differed. Most provisions I cherished were
retained, albeit in less than perfect form. For example, the
Fisher-Conable provision (above-the-line charitable deductions) was approved with a long-phased effective date.

By about 3 A.M. we had resolved all of the really tough issues except for those involving oil and commodity straddles.
When nothing came of repeated attempts at final resolution, I
became fed up and abruptly moved that the House recede on
commodity straddles. The votes were there, and we were left
with only one problem—oil. There were telephone calls to
the White House and elsewhere, and after several more hours,
that issue, too, was resolved. Exhaustion and discomfort had
accomplished, in fourteen hours, what good will and cheerful
negotiation might have done in three normal days' work.

When we had signed the conference papers, we emerged
into the morning light without much sense of mutual satisfaction, but sufficiently exhausted to realize we had been through
a debilitating experience. Both House and Senate promptly
ratified the conference report, the president signed it, and
some important tax history had been made. After thinking it
over, I realized the result was not too bad. The core of the
Reagan economic program remained intact; income tax indexing had been preserved, with a prospective effective date; the

economy would receive a good boost with a speedier depreciation system more in line with those of our international competitors, and taxpayers were getting some relief.

THE SECOND REAGAN TAX BILL

The second big tax bill of the Reagan administration was the Tax Equity and Fiscal Responsibility Act (TEFRA) of 1982. The title came from the Senate, where the substantive part of the legislation also originated. In effect, it was an effort to bring back to the Treasury some revenue lost in the great tax cuts of 1981, and it was enacted by a circuitous route, which started soon after ERTA became law.

Later, in 1981, President Reagan began talking about a need for $3 billion worth of revenue enhancement measures, which had become the great new euphemism for tax increases. The idea was that this amount, plus about $13 billion in budget cuts, would put the federal deficit at a targeted $42 billion level for fiscal 1982. I was openly and adversely critical of the move, partly because I saw no way to predict the deficit so precisely a year in advance, partly because I thought it foolish to turn around, immediately following enactment of a massive tax cut estimated at $280 billion over four years, and ask Congress to raise revenues, especially such a small amount. Many Ways and Means members were interested in taking the $3 billion out of the oil industry, and I warned the White House that if such a bill passed both Houses, as was likely if it were pursued, then the president could be faced with either vetoing the measure or alienating the southwestern Democrats who had supported him on both Gramm-Latta and Conable-Hance.

Nothing further came of the $3 billion notion that year. However, early in 1982, talk of revenue enhancement cropped up again. This time, the figure bandied about by the White House was $12 billion. At a meeting of the Republican members of Ways and Means, I asked my colleagues to let me know, by an informal show of hands, how they felt about a long list of tax

proposals that staff had prepared at our request. I was surprised to see that about $22 billion worth of "revenue enhan-
cers" might be acceptable, under certain conditions, to the
committee minority. I reported this, on a confidential basis,
to Treasury Secretary Don Regan, who showed enthusiasm
and said he would pass the word to his White House colleagues. I also showed the list to Bob Dole, who indicated he
and the Finance Committee might be moving toward development of a bill in the near future and that my information
would be helpful. I did not share the material with Dan Rostenkowski, because he already had told me that he would not
even discuss revenues with his twenty-two committee Democrats unless at least nine of our twelve Republicans had agreed
on precisely what they would support. My list was wholly informal with no pledges attached, and clearly could not satisfy
his requirement.

With Ways and Means immobilized, Bob Dole decided to
get his Finance Committee together late in June, 1982, and in
little longer than one week he completed his task. He had a
bill that raised an estimated $20 billion through a multitude of
"cats and dogs." He closed more loopholes, and ran over a
variety of constituencies in the process. Lobbying against the
Dole package was heavy from the start. Frankly, I did not believe Bob could do what he did. I thought it would take a
major energy tax to bring in $20 billion. But the Senate used
relatively little time, albeit a great deal of anguish, in approv-
ing the measure, which was tacked on to the shell of a House-
passed tariff bill, the substantive contents of which had been
absorbed in other legislation. By using a House bill, even if it
was stripped of virtually everything but the number, the Senate argued it had fulfilled the constitutional requirement that
all revenue-raising measures be initiated in the House.

By the time the Senate voted on the bill, Rostenkowski
came to me and said that although some Democrats wanted to
bypass Ways and Means and go directly to conference, he
preferred that Ways and Means live up to its responsibilities

and get started on a bill of its own. We sat down and went over some items that might be included. We worked up a list of options, but disagreed, unfortunately, on what they meant. Dan apparently thought I had agreed the committee should pass all the items on the list and that I would defend each of them to the death. I understood that we had produced a starting-point document. In any event, the day before our committee markup was scheduled, Rostenkowski held an evening caucus of his Democratic members. They were in a rebellious mood, asserting that the chairman and I had no authority to make agreements on what the House should do. Besides, they did not like the list. Next day's markup was cancelled.

At a closed committee session called rather abruptly shortly thereafter, and following a great deal of recrimination, the majority of the committee, and a few of us in the minority, voted to go to conference with the Senate without first passing a House bill. In such a case, the conference compromises would have to be between existing law and provisions of the Senate version. This was bad strategy for Republicans, although President Reagan accepted the final conference results, as did both houses. Senator Dole wanted to back off from some of the tougher provisions of the Senate bill, but Chairman Rostenkowski, with a strong majority on the House Conference Committee, held him to those provisions that were embarrassing him, and about $20 billion of additional tax revenue was recaptured. Thus, the chairman of the Ways and Means Committee cleverly eluded the coalition that had beaten him on the House floor the previous year, and made the best of a bad situation.

When a conference on TEFRA was actually started, it was once again late on a Friday. Business began at 7 P.M. and we continued throughout the night, recessing at 9:30 A.M., resuming at 2 P.M., then continuing steadily until about 2 A.M., Sunday. Like the conference on the 1981 Act, this one was a marathon. It was longer and even more frustrating for me.

One positive factor was that we met in the Ways and Means Committee's huge and relatively comfortable hearing chamber, Room–1100 in the Longworth House Office Building.

The conference ratio on our side was five to three. My own role was relatively simple. I took the position that the Senate bill, which was our only working document, preserved the essential elements of the president's program as it was contained in the 1981 Act. I worked out a coalition of business support based on my ability to effect a series of compromises, acceptable to them, on proposals to cut back even further on accelerated depreciation and to expand unemployment insurance. I managed to develop agreements that the business coalition could buy, but I took some battering in the process. Rostenkowski on several occasions was able to prevent Dole and his Senate colleagues from receding to me, with the result that I had to sign off on some provisions that fell short of desirability.

Rostenkowski exercised all the power at his disposal during the conference, a show of force that was illustrated best at the very end, when analysis showed that we had raised more money than we needed. Dole had planned, if that became the case, to back off on the size of the increase in tobacco taxes that had been incorporated in the Senate bill. He apparently had promised tobacco state senators he would do so if he could. But when he attempted to follow through, Rostenkowski announced to Dole in a loud and rather cheerful voice: "In every conference there comes a time when somebody is helpless. You are helpless now. The House recedes." Rostenkowski had the votes, with a five to three majority on the House side, and there was nothing Dole could do but acknowledge the inevitable.

When it was all over, I signed the conference report for four good reasons, as I explained to my colleagues during floor debate on the document. First, the president had asked. He laid his prestige on the line. Although I did not then, and do not now, believe in following any leader blindly, President Reagan had made what I deemed a reasonable request—to support legislation likely to improve the economy. Second, TEFRA narrowed a widening deficit gap. Third, TEFRA promised spending reductions (a promise that unfortunately never was kept). The conference report was consistent with an earlier congressional agreement to link expenditure reductions of $17 billion to the increase of revenues totaling $98 billion over a three-year span. (Again, the agreed-upon spending cut never came, but one could not know that at the time.) Finally, TEFRA preserved—against strong challenge—the indexing of marginal rates. The vote for the conference report on the House floor was not even close. Again, the president had lobbied hard and effectively with enough Republicans to supplement a sufficient number of Democratic votes.

MY LAST TAX REFORM BILL

The final reform bill on which I worked as a member of Ways and Means was the Deficit Reduction Act of 1984 (acronymed DEFRA in the fine tradition of ERTA and TEFRA). The tax reform part of DEFRA represented a small portion of its content (the conference report ran 1,151 pages), but those reforms were significant, indeed. Provisions affecting life insurance companies, alimony and other domestic relations issues, as well as numerous compliance sections, were completely rewritten for the first time. There also were many improvements in the tax treatment of pensions and tax-exempt bonds. However, as was the case with virtually all tax measures I encountered during my Ways and Means years, I had mixed feelings about the net result. It represented some significant achievements for me and a few disappointments. Understanding the reasons for both achievements and disappointments can be helped by my reviewing—in the light of nearly four years of experience—both the function of the Ways and Means Committee and my relationship with Chairman Rostenkowski.

This relationship improved a great deal during the Ninety-eighth Congress. I attributed that both to Dan's success and to his decency. It also reflected (1) his basic lack of substantive interest in the tax law, (2) what I perceived to be his growing acceptance of my legislative role, and (3) his reduced fear that I might be able to ambush him through floor reversal of committee action, after the 1982 election had sapped the strength of conservatives in the House as a whole. The chairman had also cemented control of his committee. He did this in a number of interesting and, to some degree, unpleasant ways.

First, Mr. Rostenkowski used a surprising vindictiveness against those who crossed him. He was never vindictive toward me, because he expected nothing but political opposition from me, but someone like Kent Hance found himself virtually isolated on the committee because of his cooperation in the 1981 act. At one point, Kent got all the way to the airport before he discovered that the chairman had not signed his travel vouchers to go to China with the Trade Subcommittee. The message was clear that the memory of the chairman was long. Functioning in a committee where the leader has such power to cause personal embarrassment and unpleasantness for a recalcitrant member can be very difficult.

Second, Dan raised a large campaign chest, probably for many purposes, but among others to permit him to contribute political campaign funds to cooperating members of his committee when they ran for reelection. He certainly was not the first to do this, nor will he be the last. In my opinion, this has become a deplorably acceptable device for leadership in both parties. This provides a maintenance of election funds from which contributions can be made to special friends and cooperating colleagues when they run for reelection to leadership roles in the House. This creates financial obligations on which the leader can base continuing support.

Third, he used a most interesting device for the real world of legislation. He developed an arrangement, spoken or unspoken, with his subcommittee chairmen: Sam Gibbons, of Florida, on Trade; Jake Pickle, of Texas, on Oversight; Charlie Rangel, of New York, on Select Revenue Measures; and Pete Stark, of California, on Health. This arrangement was one whereby he agreed to support without question whatever they brought out of their subcommittees, in return for their willingness to go along with what he wanted in conference committees, where the aim ostensibly is supposed to be to resolve the final form of legislation that has been passed in varying versions by House and Senate. These five members, who now habitually make up the House Conference Committee cadre on most revenue bills, served as a phalanx, on whose spears diverse Republicans of the House and distinguished members of the Senate Finance Committee threw themselves before they retreated, bleeding and defeated. There can be any number of conferees, but that five-to-three solid bloc from the House usually has held sway.

Critical details of important legislation are written in conference, anyway, not in committee and not on either floor. As long as Rostenkowski had this firm agreement with his subcommittee chairmen, he could dominate conferences even against as effective a legislator as Bob Dole. Time and again Sam Gibbons or Jake Pickle has said to me in the course of a conference: "Barber, we agree with you about this matter, but we promised Danny we wouldn't rock the boat." In return, Dan became more of a free trader at the behest of Sam Gibbons, a tough guy on Social Security at the behest of Jake Pickle, or a big, social welfare man to support Charlie Rangel, or unconventional on health bills to fit Pete Stark. He rarely took a larger contingent to a conference committee because that would require him to include two Democrats he could not depend upon so readily—Andy Jacobs of Indiana, a bright, but unpredictable man, and Jim Jones,* whose entre-

---

*Jim Jones subsequently ran unsuccessfully for the Senate and thus lost his House seat.

preneurial style and chairmanship of the Budget Committee made him strongly suspect in terms of loyalty and protection of Ways and Means turf.

In short, in the Ninety-eighth Congress, Dan Rostenkowski came into full control of the Ways and Means Committee. This didn't mean that he was anxious to win every point, but only that he was anxious to win those points that fell into the primary province of politics. To him, a major function of politics is control, a natural attitude for somebody originally coming out of the Daley organization in Chicago. I found that as long as he had control, and as long as I did not cross him on those issues involving politics of the Democratic Party, and particularly politics of committee jurisdiction, he would acknowledge my legislative hobbies, my substantive interests, and would be perfectly willing to throw me a bone now and then. In this environment, the most important decisions I had to make related to the bones that I thought I could get the chairman to throw me and a careful analysis of sensitivities surrounding his leadership.

With particular respect to the 1984 tax act, he had several real concerns. Foremost among them was his great contest with members of the Rules Committee (notably Martin Frost of Texas) over his efforts to "cap" state use of tax-exempt bonds in the general area of revenue bonding of industrial developments. He was determined to win and ultimately did, although he was forced to compromise it on a number of occasions. I stood shoulder to shoulder with him on this issue and he seemed to appreciate that.

Another issue that greatly concerned him was the president's enterprise zone proposals, which would, in effect, have given tax breaks to urban restorations. I suspect he resented this program because he did not want to help Jack Kemp, who assumed paternity of the plan, and because of macro-political and constituency policies of Ronald Reagan's efforts to do something for poor people. Dan didn't take on this issue directly, but gave a proxy to Charlie Rangel, a man who didn't want Ronald Reagan to do anything for his Harlem constituents, either, and who, through a series of ploys, constantly prevented legislation from being seriously considered by the Ways and Means Committee.

The Reagan administration asked me to be the prime sponsor of enterprise zone legislation and I did everything I could to advance it, realizing that it was more political than substantive. I made the assessment, early on, that it was unlikely we would be able to succeed, considering the formidable opposition, and so I treated it like a political issue, in a manner that I thought Rostenkowski could understand, playing the game openly with him in a way that would not become personal. Predictably, enterprise zones were "killed" at the end of the 1984 conference by a miscalculation on the Senate's part. In effect, the Senate participants agreed prematurely to drop it as a conference item because they thought it could be revived later. It never was.

Rostenkowski also had some interest in advancing his "freeze" proposal. Originally he espoused a plan to "freeze" several prospective tax law changes, which would, in effect, keep some key 1981 changes from taking effect as scheduled. For instance, he had wanted to freeze income tax indexing and the entire estate tax liberalization enacted in ERTA. He backed off on these particular provisions, although he retained an estate tax rate freeze that was compromised in conference. I opposed him vigorously on this matter, along with the administration. But when he compromised his stand, I stopped giving him a tough time, deeming that raising some money as part of the deficit reduction package would be desirable; several of his freeze proposals were most helpful in this respect.

As to the DEFRA items in which I was personally most interested, the first was something called DISC-FISC. The Domestic International Sales Corporation (DISC), a tax preference encouraging exports rather than American investment in subsidiaries abroad, had been on our law books for about ten years. Through a series of miscalculations and heel-draggings, the United States allowed itself to be backed into a corner by the European community, which claimed that DISC was illegal under GATT (General Agreement on Tariffs and Trade). To avoid the consequences of this illegality, the United States finally agreed to change the DISC in a way that might make it legal under GATT. We did this through a complex measure known as the Foreign International Sales Corporation (FISC). Although its GATT legality is questionable, America has more or less an unspoken agreement with the Europeans that they will not challenge it.

Most large American companies and many small ones have used DISC to provide a modest tax deferral on profits made abroad through the export of American-made goods. At the time the deferral was put in place, there was an unspoken agreement that taxes so deferred would be deferred indefinitely. Money from the deferral, of course, had to be invested in export facilities abroad, or in the development of trade-related assets, which would extend our trade outreach. On repeal of the DISC provisions, and the substitution of the alternative FISC procedures, allegations surfaced that the United States should collect deferred taxes, and indeed my former colleague, Pete Stark, made this a major campaign during the conference on the 1984 act in which FISC was substituted. His plan would have had a devastating impact on the earnings statements of many corporations, and in my view would have been an unjustified reversal of the understanding about indefinite deferral that all the participants had when DISC was first put on the books. Stark talked about it as a "giveaway" of $10 billion to our richest corporations. Dan was very nervous about this, but he did listen to my strong representations and did note my unwavering opposition to Stark in private discussions. In the end, he helped our cause prevail. To have done anything else, in my view, would have been disastrous—not just for corporate earnings statements for the foreseeable future, but would have greatly affected the willingness of American companies to export when the dollar was so strong. Given our imbalance of trade this would have been foolish.

The second item on which I had a rather interesting success had to do with a Gibbons-Conable proposal that would have repealed the 30 percent withholding tax on foreign investments in this country. Such a tax had been on the books for some time, and although I got the repeal to the floor of the House once before, it was defeated at that time by those who claimed that I was trying to treat foreigners too well. The problem is that the United States was (and still is) relying on heavy foreign investment to offset in current payments the very serious imbalance of trade. Inevitably, at some point the dollar will decline in value and a reverse flow of capital will result, putting great pressure on interest rates and the value of the dollar. Unfortunately, the offsetting competitiveness of American trade goods is not likely to be statistically evident until later, and so the sudden outflow of foreign investment from the United States could create very serious fiscal repercussions.

Sam Gibbons' cosponsorship gave my proposal some bipartisan credibility, but we had a big fight over the extent to which repeal of the withholding would impact the Netherlands Antilles, the window through which American borrowers could get access to the European dollar market. Large corporations could set up shell subsidiaries in the Netherlands Antilles to issue bonds in the European dollar market, but more general accessibility to this large sum of dollar credits in Europe was not possible as long as the holders were subject to withholding of American tax. Other countries do not have such withholding, and I argued that this pool of capital could go a long way toward taking pressure off interest rates in the American market, which otherwise would depend only on the domestic dollar pool for its borrowings. The question of whether such bonds should be in bearer form, or registered, greatly complicated the initiative, since there were those who claimed that Americans could borrow abroad and get the advantage of bearer securities, of which no record was kept, for tax evasion purposes. The Senate tried to phase down the withholding tax, which would have been totally ineffective, at the same time causing problems for the Netherlands Antilles. In conference, we compromised the issue by making it prospective only with respect to future bond issues, but clearly it has had a salubrious effect already on the size of the potential loan pool for both American private and public debtors. Fortunately, Rostenkowski did not feel strongly about this, and did not oppose me on it. It was adopted, and I was able to assume a large part of the credit for having successfully maneuvered a compromise through conference.

A third item of special interest to me had to do with Section 125 of the Internal Revenue Code, which deals with pension "cafeteria" plans. This form of fringe benefit was offered to employees on an alternative basis, allowing them to choose among several different types according to their needs. This kind of plan was designed in particular to help women who have special needs for day care, but only for limited periods of time and, in unusual cases, and to permit some alternative to top-dollar health insurance benefits if employees would rather have some other benefit.

The cafeteria plan device had been authorized by law for nearly six years before Treasury issued regulations. It had been giving informal advice to corporations inquiring about the issue, indicating that certain types of alternative plans were perfectly acceptable. Many corporations began using cafeteria plan benefits, only to find early in 1984 that Treasury had put out a press release saying regulations would be issued to stop, retroactively, certain practices that Treasury perceived to be abusive in the cafeteria plan area. Apparently regulations, which were issued shortly after the press release, might require reissuance of amended tax returns for about two million employees, probably shortly before the next election. I thought Treasury was not only shooting itself in the foot, but in a vital organ, since this action was politically un-wise and frustrated the intent of Congress, which was quite clear with respect to cafeteria plans. Before the conference was a proposal permitting continuance of cafeteria plans for a reasonable period of time until the whole subject could be more carefully reviewed. Eventually this modest compromise was accepted and cafeteria plans have been saved, at least for the time being, despite opposition of Treasury and the IRS. The fourth item interesting me particularly was a liberaliza-tion of foundation regulations, which had been quite punitive and discouraging to foundation creation ever since the 1969 Tax Act. The DEFRA legislation offered some important im-provement in this area.

These four items, DISC-FISC, withholding on foreign in-vestments, cafeteria plans, and liberalization of foundation regulations, were, in my view, major accomplishments in the 1984 Tax Act for which I took some credit. I could not have accomplished this without the help, or at least the forebear-ance, of Chairman Rostenkowski, and so I clearly had no rea-son to complain about his willingness at least to allow me some leeway in the environment of the Ninety-eighth Con-gress. Repeating my assessment of him—his word is good and he is intellectually capable of understanding any issue that comes before the committee. He is a decent man, anxious to do a good job.

Now, let me deal, finally, with some of the disappointments I had in the 1984 tax act. One of these had to do with Senator Russell Long's well-known hobby—ESOP's or Employee Stock Option Plans, whereby the employees of a company can gradually acquire ownership of the company through tax credits, which Russell has, over the years, gotten into the law so as to give preference to such purchases. He offered some additional, controversial tax preferences to beef up the ESOP proposal and this became a sore point in the DEFRA confer-ence. There was general outrage that Russell was seeking to make ESOPs even more favored at other taxpayers' expense.

Dan Rostenkowski admitted to me at the beginning of the conference that he had committed himself personally to Russell on this issue, but indicated he would not be heartbroken if it did not succeed. A check of other House conferees showed that we were evenly divided, since Russell had done his homework well. I suggested to others in opposition that the only way we could deal with Russell would be to face him down as a group and that we should meet with him. The others agreed and I set up such a meeting. I was the only one who showed up. When I explained what I was there for, he said to me, "Barber, the one thing consistent about your service in Congress is your absolutely implacable hostility to ESOPs. I can never understand that."

I tried to explain my view of the substance of his proposal—i.e., that employees might find an unscrupulous employer using it as a device for financing his failing business, thus giving the employees illusory security and ultimately leaving them holding the bag. He waved such concerns aside and said he would beat me yet. He did. Late in the morning of an all-night conference session, one of my fellow holdouts told me he had to knuckle under. He said Russell had wakened him while he was sleeping on his office sofa, and kept pulling the handkerchief shielding his eyes away from his face until he agreed to change his position. This is a good example of the absolute single-mindedness of Russell Long's persistent quest. We lost a vote and the ball game.

As to the enterprise zone proposal, it also went down in defeat. However, I doubt that America has heard the last of it. I still believe this to be a good, yet primarily a political issue. In the right form, it is creative federalism at its best. On balance, however, the 1984 tax bill was acceptable. It became controversial primarily because of the fiscal overtones. It was part of a deficit reduction package that probably never will achieve on the expenditure side what was achieved on the tax side, and, therefore, it contributed one more element to the asymmetrical congressional effort at deficit reduction. Many provisions in it were absolutely necessary, however. In addition to those already mentioned, there was termination of a moratorium concerning non-statutory fringe benefits. There were some modest reductions in Medicare and Medicaid expenditures, although the need for a comprehensive resolution of our problems in public health programs remained, and still looms.

Overall, I still think it was a good measure on which to terminate my tax-writing career. I was pleased with my role and felt that my successes outweighed my failures, even though not by a wide margin. In joining a majority of the House to adopt the omnibus measure, I felt comfortable with my vote, but a bit frustrated with being unable to accomplish more. Legislating, though, is like that, especially in the tax area, where virtually every provision is complicated. Many, many times I have stood on the floor of the House and explained my support for a Ways and Means bill by noting that it fell far short of perfection, that it included some provisions that were particularly painful to me, but that it did have some good parts, and that as a whole it was a step in the right direction.

Ways and Means bills rarely could be painted boldly in black or white. Because of their complex contents, they usually were shrouded in grey, causing our minds to be, as Hamlet put it, "sicklied o'er with the pale cast of thought." Tax reform has never brought pure happiness. It always was a product of compromise. Getting something meant giving up something. Early in my committee career, I had to decide—as all of us had to decide—whether I would be an absolute purist and decline to participate in the give and take of compromise, thus remaining immaculately unproductive, or whether I would become a willing participant and work hard to get the very best results I could. For me, the choice was easy, even if the participation was not.

Given my background and my strong views on tax matters, how would I have handled the 1986 Reform Act? I really cannot answer with certainty, because I was not there. I was not in the Ways and Means boiler room watching the engine turn over. I don't and won't speculate on that. What I can do, and will do, is appraise that landmark legislation from the viewpoint of an outsider with some insider experience.

CHAPTER 4

THE 1986 ACT: AN APPRAISAL

THE TAX REFORM ACT of 1986 had a strange history. Its evolution formed an unusual, if not unique, chapter in the annals of major income tax revision. First of all, there was no clearly visible groundswell of public support for the legislation. Oh, there were some rallies and some editorials, and some television hoopla. However, there was no mass movement, constantly applying pressure for action. Most people are for tax reform, of course, but probably in concept only. If you ask them—and many polltakers did so while the bill was taking shape—they will tell you that the existing system needs reforming. But if your questions run deep, you will get a mixed, and perhaps an inconsistent, set of responses.

I always have felt—based on my conversations with varied constituencies on the subject over the past twenty-five years—that most taxpayers want reform only if it means either (1) they will pay less in taxes or (2) someone they know and believe to be much wealthier and devious will pay more. I suspect that many of the responses given to pollsters on the 1986 act, as it developed, were based on those kinds of feelings. In any event, tens of millions of people did not rise up, at any given time, to give the 1986 reform a ringing endorsement. When the president made public appearances during this period, and delivered speeches on the subject, his audiences did cheer mightily. They probably would, however, have reached the same way to virtually any message from this extraordinarily popular leader. Members of Congress, whose job it was to dispose of the legislation by moving forward with it or scrapping it, have told me that their mail from constituents on tax reform never grew unusually heavy during the period. The pressure to act favorably "never came from home, it came from here" (meaning Washington), a congressional friend remarked one day in summing up the phenomenon.

A second unusual factor in the evolution of tax reform, 1986 style, was the sporadic or lukewarm support it received from national leaders. The president asked for it, and periodically "took to the stump" for it. But there were times when he appeared to be, at the very least, apathetic. Congressional backing also was inconsistent. The Speaker of the House always said he favored tax reform, because it had been a feature of Democratic Party platforms for years. Yet I had the feeling that he was somewhat queasy about the details as they unfolded.

Chairman of the House tax-writing committee, Dan Rostenkowski, clearly was not a devotee of intricate tax revision, but he saw very clearly that if the Democrats did not act positively they could, in effect, cede to the Republican president all the political advantage that might accrue in pushing tax reform as a concept. On the Republican side of the House, the leadership initially had a negative attitude. An exception was Jack Kemp, chairman of the Republican conference, but he later recoiled when he saw what the Democratic-packed Ways and Means Committee had presented as tax reform. In the Senate, ardent advocates of reform were even fewer in number.

So how did the legislation survive? With no massive and steady demand from the electorate, and with such wavering support from the leadership of both parties, how could a major overhaul of the nation's income tax structure take place? The answer is complex, although not nearly as much so as the legislation itself. Perhaps it can be seen more easily through the sequence of events leading up to its enactment. Like a flower, it may be more fully appraised and understood as its petals unfold.

The first petal unfolded in a flurry of rhetoric during the 1984 presidential campaign. Of course, both major parties had called for tax reform of sorts in their political platforms, but the first burst really came, it seems to me, when the president and his advisers decided how to deal with the tax issue *vis-à-vis* the Democratic challenger, Walter Mondale. Mondale had called for tax increases, and the Reagan team immediately realized the advantage that gave them in courting public opinion. They reasoned quite correctly that very few Americans get wildly enthusiastic about the prospect of paying higher taxes. Furthermore, they did not want to say absolutely nothing on the issue. After all, the question of fairness had been raised. Mr. Mondale had indicated he had higher taxes in mind only for the rich. He said the less-well-off were carrying too much of the nation's revenue load already, and something ought to be done about it.

By way of response, President Reagan continued to press home the point that he opposed tax increases *per se.* In fact, he was not only in favor of lower taxes for all, but actually had done something about it in his first four years via the Conable-Hance/Kemp-Kasten vehicle, which lowered marginal rates for individuals by 25 percent. He also—to show continued action on this front—asked his Treasury Secretary, Don Regan, to start a new study on tax policy with the aim of getting those rates even lower. Don Regan turned the task over to his skilled and inventive assistants in the Treasury Department.

Now, it is true that the top tier of his assistants were presidential appointees, naturally anxious to please the president and their more immediate boss. But even they, at least some of them, had their own agendas, and they also were not of one mind on tax policy. Some of them were wedded to a basic "supply side" theory of economics, which held that the only reform really essential was a drastic further lowering of tax rates. Some of them were not so certain. And some preferred lowering the deficit to lowering taxes further.

Under them all was a veritable army of professional bureaucrats. Many of these had labored long in the Treasury vineyard, dreaming of the day when they might be directed to develop a major tax reform package. They had been furtively working on this for years, of course, and their bottom desk drawers were jammed with cherished schemes. Many of them probably never really thought their dream would come true but—*mirabile dictu!*—they were cleared for action.

Some of these departmental professionals had been greatly influenced by the late Stanley Surrey, a Harvard Law School professor, who was assistant secretary for tax policy from 1961 to 1969. Surrey had definite ideas on just how the tax code should be reformed. In a very small nutshell, he believed that our income tax system should be used only to raise revenues and that the rate of taxation should be highly progressive. He did not favor "tax incentives" which he called instead "tax expenditures" on the theory that every preference eroded revenues otherwise available to the government. His ideas represented radically progressive income redistribution as far as most tax policy conservatives were concerned. There was more to it, of course, but that was the core of the Surrey school, which has always had a large student body, both inside and outside of Treasury.

The Surrey school was frustrated for decades. It could not get anywhere with its reforming zeal under *any* administration, Republican *or* Democratic. Suddenly, it was a Republican president, considered by them a right-wing one at that, who told the Surrey disciples and other reformers in the Treasury Department that it was all right to bring their old ideas out of the dark recesses, to dust them off, and to offer them as part of a new reform package. "Reduce the rates," they were told, "even by eliminating tax incentives if necessary."

The result, brought forth by Don Regan and company in

November of 1984 (after the election), was a proposal that came to be known in some quarters as Treasury I. It was a mix of old and new reform ideas, but the tilt definitely was toward redistributing income largely at the expense of the country's industrial base. Treasury I caused such a ruckus among the president's closest supporters and advisers that it was rather hastily withdrawn for repairs. A new and improved model, toned either down or up depending on one's point of view, was presented to the world in May, 1985. This one, with a few modifications, was labeled "The President's Tax Reform Proposals to the Congress for Fairness, Growth, and Simplicity." It also was known as Treasury II or White House I. Modifications prior to presentation were made, I suspect, under the primary direction of the White House Chief of Staff, James E. Baker III, just before he left that post in a dramatic exchange of jobs with Treasury Secretary Regan. I also suspect that Jim was assisted actively in this "modifying" endeavor by Richard Darman, who went with Baker to Treasury as deputy secretary.

Essentially, the president's package called for three marginal rates of 15, 25, and 35 percent as compared with fifteen rates ranging from 11 to 50 percent. The loss of revenue through rate reduction was covered in large part through repeal of deductions for state and local taxes and through removing investment incentives, such as eliminating the investment tax credit and gutting the liberalized depreciation provisions of the Conable-Hance bill. You can imagine my general view of the latter change. In sum, the president's package shifted an estimated $120 billion of the tax burden from individuals to business enterprises, including many corporations.

Corporate America was split widely on tax reform as a result. Many business leaders, smitten by the promise of a 33 percent maximum corporate rate in years ahead, when they were hoping to have higher profits, jumped on the tax reform bandwagon early, and stayed there throughout the process. Clearly, many of these executives who had staggeringly high personal salaries, also focused their attention on the potential for greatly enhanced individual take-home pay as well as well as on the impact the package would have on business investment and business tax burdens. There were, of course, a group of business people who counted heavily on the ITC and more rapid write-offs for plant expansion and improvements, and these people quickly went on the defensive. Most individual taxpayers were, I think, dazzled and perhaps temporarily blinded by a sparkling array of statistics and rhetoric, both praising and condemning the new tax reform effort. They liked what they heard about lower rates, but they were alarmed at the prospect of losing some cherished deductions.

Dan Rostenkowski moved quickly to make sure that if tax reform did find favor with a majority of voters, the Democratic Party would get at least some of the credit. In a well-received response to the president's address announcing tax reform, and later, in a statement opening public hearings on the subject before his Ways and Means Committee, he restated his party's claim to tax reform as a political issue. He went back to a statement by Harry Truman on fairness to do so. He then pledged his own personal commitment to lead the charge in the House of Representatives. The Ways and Means Committee opened its hearings on May 30, 1985, two days after the president's nationwide address on his tax plan. The series was closed two months later on July 31. There was little testimony presented that should have surprised the members. One after another, spokespersons marched to the witness table to declare that tax reform would destroy their world or make it even better.

Actual mark-up of a committee bill started on September 18, and continued, in fits and starts, until December 3, 1985. The president and his aides, notably Don Regan and Jim Baker, had to realize what they were up against when the legislative mill began grinding away at their proposal. There was no realistic way that Dan Rostenkowski and the Democrats were going to give them what they wanted. The result out of committee obviously would be a bill with an indelible Democratic stamp on it, so as to ensure majority party backing on the floor of the House at voting time. There was little room for erosion of support. A coalition of conservative Democrats and disgruntled Republicans could sink the reform effort, and Rostenkowski made sure the president got the message: "You might not love the committee bill, but if it goes down to defeat, your drive for tax reform goes down with it, because the Republican majority in the Senate will not take up a lost cause."

The Committee bill was, indeed, not to the president's liking. It offered top rates of 38 percent for individuals and shifted even more of the total tax burden to business and industry, for example, by retaining deductions for state and local taxes while further emasculating depreciation provisions. The bill also was disliked by most House Republicans and by numerous Democrats, who did indeed put together a coalition not unlike the ones that had brought victory to the president in his first-term efforts at budget-and-tax cutting. Despite this history, leaders on both sides of the aisle reportedly were shocked when, on December 10, 1985, a key procedural vote on the rule (a House resolution governing debate on the bill itself) went against the proponents by 223 to 202.

A dismayed White House staff quickly regrouped, seeking recovery advice from House Republican leaders. After much consultation, a decision was made to have the president pledge to unhappy members that he would not sign into law *any* tax reform bill that failed to include "pro-family" and certain other provisions, most notably lower rates. He did this in a rare personal appearance at a large rally in the Rayburn House Office Building. This dramatic move turned the tide. Jack Kemp, House Republican Whip Trent Lott, and other leaders disgusted with the Ways and Means bill agreed to support it under the president's new condition. Thus, when the rule came up again, on December 17, the vote was overwhelmingly the other way (258–168) and the game was over. Next stop for the bill was the Senate.

The chairman of Ways and Means' counterpart, the Senate Finance Committee, was Bob Packwood of Oregon, who moved up when Bob Dole moved out to become Senate Majority Leader. Bob Packwood was not enamored of the tax reform effort in general or of the House product in particular. He had said as much on several occasions. However, between the time the House disgorged its bill and the Finance Committee began its markup, on March 19, 1986, he had a different perspective. He had come to grips with the fact that, as chairman of the committee charged with the responsibility of taking action, he was bound to lead the way. He really had no choice.

The rest is legislative legend. The bill, it is said, lay near death in the Finance Committee as it had in Ways and Means, until Packwood and his chief assistant decided one day to propose lowering the top marginal rate to 27 percent and coupling that with a bottom rate of 15 percent. The decision was part inspiration and part desperation, or so it was said. In any case, the lower rates were credited with winning the day for tax reform in the Senate. The bill cleared the committee twenty to zero and the Floor ninety-seven to three.

The final result, reached after a hectic Senate-House conference, met the president's basic requirements and retained the most ballyhooed other provisions of both House and Senate bills. For example, there was retention of the deduction for state and local income and property taxes (from the House) and low maximum rates of 28 percent for individuals and 34 percent for corporations (from the Senate). The president soon signed the conference report into law in a great outdoor ceremony at the White House. Some members of Congress already had gone home to campaign for reelection and the Speakers' platform held some members who had not been especially close to the tax reform effort. It really didn't matter. Everyone smiled broadly, and the president left the podium to hearty applause from the audience, composed largely of staff and lobbyists.

Among many other things, the new law establishes several guidelines. It phases in marginal tax rates of 15 percent up to 28 percent. Starting in 1987, the top rate drops from 50 percent to 38.5 percent and tax brackets are reduced in number from fifteen to five. Perhaps not entirely understood by many taxpayers, however, is a "bubble" effect, which makes the top effective rate 33 percent for many taxpayers. This occurs because the 15 percent rate applies to taxable income up to $29,750 for married couples, $23,900 for heads of households, or $17,850 for single persons. The 28 percent rate applies to other taxable income, *except* that the 15 percent rate is phased out for certain higher income taxpayers—married couples with incomes between $71,900 and $149,250, heads of household with incomes between $61,650 and $123,790, and single taxpayers with incomes between $43,150 and $89,560. The net effect of this is a 5 percent surtax on incomes in those ranges.

Changes increase personal exemptions for many taxpayers to $1,900 in 1987, $1,950 in 1988, and $2,000 in 1989. After that, the exemption will be adjusted according to increases in the consumer price index. Personal exemption is phased out for those with taxable incomes over $147,250 for married couples, $123,790 for heads of household, and $89,560 for single taxpayer. The zero bracket amount is replaced (the threshold of taxation) with a standard deduction for non-itemizers equal to $5,000 (marrieds), $4,400 (heads of household), and $2,500 (singles), with these amounts indexed to inflation starting in 1989.

The law repeals the lower rate (20 percent maximum) for capital gains, now taxable as ordinary income, at a top rate of 28 percent (33 percent for those with incomes just below the top levels). It repeals (on a phased-out basis) deductions for consumer interest, and limits deductions for mortgage interest to first and second houses. It severely limits the deduction for contributions to individual retirement accounts (IRAs). A

$2,000 deduction still can be taken, and thus deferred for tax purposes, by taxpayers with adjusted gross incomes up to $40,000 for joint filers and $25,000 for single filers. The deduction is phased out over those income thresholds. It limits deductions for interest on investments to amounts equal to net investment income. It cuts the top corporate rate from 46 percent to 40 percent in 1987, for calendar year filers, and to 34 percent thereafter.

It tightens the rates for taxation of employee benefits and qualified retirement plans. Under the new law, employee-welfare plans must be examined carefully to see if they meet anti-discrimination rules effective in 1988. Employer costs are likely to rise for welfare and fringe benefit plans. Also, starting in 1987, the maximum salary-reduction dollar limit for 401(k) plans drops from $30,000 to $7,000

The law repeals the investment tax credit and provides for longer depreciation periods for most assets (but larger deductions in early years for short-lived assets). The result is that the new depreciation system does not make up for loss of the ITC, even in the case of manufacturing equipment for which the write-off may be more generous. It also repeals the above-the-line charitable tax deduction for non-itemizers.

In effect, the new 1986 Internal Revenue Code would lower total individual income taxes by an estimated $122 billion over the five-year period through 1991, and transfer that burden to the corporate side of the ledger. Major increases for individual taxpayers will come via the new, restrictive rules on tax shelters and interest expense, and the new treatment of pension and employee benefit income ($41.6 billion through 1991). Limiting passive losses to net investment income, for example, would yield an estimated $67.2 billion in added revenue over the period. Repealing the investment tax credit and changing depreciation rules should now bring in an estimated $119 billion.

The magnitude of the changes effected by the new law is difficult to comprehend readily. One stated objective of the exercise was to reduce the role of taxation in both individual and business planning, to force us all to make our monetary decisions for economic and not for tax policy considerations. In the process, many of the old "preferences" have been eliminated or curtailed in use. Some of the more popular ones (mortgage interest, state and local income, and property taxes) were retained in large part simply because passage of the package in House and Senate was deemed to be impossible otherwise.

Also in the process, very tough minimum taxes, for both individuals and corporations, have been instituted. Again, a stated objective was to enhance the "fairness" concept, to make sure that virtually everyone pays *some* tax. For individuals, the minimum tax rate is boosted from 20 percent to 21 percent and the items on which it is levied are increased substantially in number and breadth, with the expected result that revenue from this source will rise by nearly $4 billion in 1988, and by more than $8 billion through 1991. A new corporate minimum will bring in an anticipated $22 billion over the same five-year period.

The changes were designed, its planners said, to make certain that all "economic" income is subject to an effective tax rate close to the highest marginal rate. Given, then, the sheer magnitude of the legislation, the high degree of uncertainty about its impact, and its somewhat shaky support from both the electorate and political leaders, how did it survive and become law? A short answer might well be that its instigators, however reticent any one of them might have been at times, came through at critical moments to breathe new life into the project. The president, who started the reform ball rolling, temporarily withheld support as the bill came out of the Ways and Means Committee, but later put his prestige on the line with a blatant personal appeal to his fellow Republicans to keep the process alive, to get the bill through the House and move it to the Senate for corrective surgery.

Dan Rostenkowski, who seemed on the verge of abandoning the whole idea when his committee voted narrowly against limiting certain special rules for banks (the reserve method for bad debts), a proposition worth about $5 billion over five years), somehow negotiated a reconsideration of the vote and won a comparably narrow victory the second time around. It was enough to give him, and the bill, a second wind. Bob Packwood, faced with negative reactions whether he looked to the right or the left on his Finance Committee, gambled and won on a sudden shift to dramatically lower rates.

If there were *any* ever-present forces to assist the principal players at critical times, and to provide a consistency of support throughout the process, they were Secretary Baker and his deputy, Dick Darman, plus a business leadership group operating as the Tax Reform Coalition (TRAC). The former pair, good political operatives, saw their own careers at stake. The latter group was made up of organizations, both large and small, that saw an overriding benefit in lower marginal rates.

Jim Baker had much to do with keeping the White House establishment from backing off the project entirely. While he was the president's chief of staff, he (and Darman) helped redirect Treasury I and massage Treasury II until it became White House I. When the bill came to Congress, he (with Darman) hovered over it, day by day. They talked incessantly to members, especially doubtful ones, provided reassurances, and sufficient prompting for key players in the game. Baker had the marvelous ability to make every legislator feel like "one of Jim's closest friends." Darman was doggedly persistent. He had answers when they were needed, and he was Baker's alter ego. He was referred to variously during the process as "the Darth Vader of tax reform" and "Jim's American Express card," because Baker never left home without him.

Another important protagonist in the 1985–86 tax reform story was, as indicated earlier, Stanley Surrey. He laid a policy foundation for the effort two decades earlier, and had established a following in the bureaucracy that seized an opportunity when it was offered. He was a shadowy player in the game, but I think it is fair to say that the Internal Revenue Code of 1986 reflects his philosophy in very substantial and distinctive ways. The new law does essentially what he would have wanted it to do. It makes the income tax structure less an economic or social force and more a revenue-raising engine. It redistributes income, extensively and specifically, from businesses to individuals, and in many instances, from higher to lower income groups.

Are such changes good or bad? Will they benefit some taxpayers to the detriment of others? Will they help or hinder the United States in global marketplaces? We will not—we cannot—measure the new law's impact in any of these respects, with any degree of real accuracy, until enough time has elapsed so the changes can be viewed in the light of practical experience. We will not have any reliable answers until we can exercise hindsight.

My own general views, however (with great forebearance), should be reasonably clear to my colleagues, who have listened to me over the years. These are clear in lectures I have given in the Rothbaum series, delivered long before this tax reform epic built up a head of steam, and upon which much of this text is based. I doubt that the 1986 Code will, of itself, bring either depression or expansion. It probably will offer relief to some Americans, especially low-income people who are dropped from tax rolls because of it. It is not likely to be a boon to entrepreneurs, risk-taking investors among us. It will tax capital-intensive industries more heavily, and could put a damper on real estate, public utility, and transportation enterprises. Jobs will be lost as a result, but other jobs may be created in retail and wholesale businesses, in large and technologically-oriented firms, and in non-electrical machinery manufacturing companies—all of which should be better off, at least in the short term.

The new law is not, I fear, destined greatly to stimulate our total domestic savings. Some think it will. I do not. I have never believed that reducing marginal tax rates would encourage savings half as efficiently as specific savings preferences will. For most taxpayers, the changes will be a boon to consumption, rather than savings. Because our capital requirements ultimately should be financed with domestic (rather than foreign) savings, I doubt that our overall competitive position in world markets will be enhanced. I yearn to see our tax incentives on the side of savings and investment, rather than consumption. We are already over-consumers.

However, I am not so pessimistic for the long run. In the first place, looking at the new tax law as a permanent structure is foolish. Just as the 1913 Act remained pristine for a very short time, and just as the Internal Revenue Code of 1954 was "improved" frequently, so the 1986 Code will be changed periodically. The urge for tax preferences springs eternal in the legislator's sympathetic heart. The only certainty about the new law is that it offers very little certainty to taxpayers in the future.

The president's tax reform proposal, as it was sent to Congress in the first place, was said to promote fairness, growth, and simplicity. The final result may be perceived as more fair by some observers, or as economically stimulating by others. There clearly are mixed reviews on both points. I cannot imagine anyone seeing it as less complicated. Simple it is not. As taxpayers began wrestling with the new forms and requirements in 1988, the first tax-year in which the changes really become effective *en masse*, they may have found more complications than they anticipated, prompting more complaints than usual. The spring of 1988 may have been a difficult period for members of Congress and for the IRS. Before you know it, dismayed taxpayers will be asking, once again, for a new round of tax reform. There we go, again.

CHAPTER 5

GETTING AND SPENDING:
AN OVERVIEW

FOR MANY YEARS, as a member of Congress with a reputation for being somewhat conservative on fiscal matters, I went around telling everyone that federal deficits could kill us. If unchecked, I argued, they could wreak havoc with our economy, and pose serious problems for our allies and trading partners as well. In more recent years, however, I found myself surrounded by a large group of fellow Republicans who also claim to be fiscal conservatives, but who have told me not to worry so much about deficits. If we keep them caged, according to them, even though they are huge, they won't kill. I must say that even my party leader, the president, has made that point. Well, I also am a realist and while I remain fearful of monstrous deficits, I must admit that they have grown a lot and we are not dead yet.

Another aspect of the continuing deficit debate that bemuses me is that what they say on the subject no longer can distinguish Republicans from Democrats. There was a time when Democrats, with the usual far-left exceptions, weren't terribly worried about consequences of spending. Today, some of the fiercest arguments for fiscal restraint come from that side of the political aisle. In fairness, I should acknowledge that the reverse is true of many Republicans. One fact I have observed with more than passing interest is that much of this change in political attitudes, or perhaps I should say, in politicians' attitudes, toward our fiscal policy became most noticeable starting about 1980. The date is not purely coincidental. The major shift in political focus on fiscal policy is directly traceable, I think, to the arrival of this administration. Credit, or blame, is easy to pin down.

The title of this section is "Getting and Spending." One well might wonder why that particular choice of words. It goes back to my college days and words of poet William Wordsworth. I particularly liked one of his sonnets, that begins: "The world is too much with us; late and soon, / Getting and spending, we lay waste our powers." I thought of that phrase in this connection, because fiscal policy is too much with us in Congress, and the getting and spending aspects of fiscal policy has come to be a brooding presence in Washington.

Congress spends a great deal of its time specifically worrying about fiscal policy. Look what happens whenever the statutory limit on the public debt needs to be raised and there is a separate and clear vote on that one issue. Members, especially those in opposition, rise to rhetorical heights. I am sure all those earnest congressmen and senators are going to be embroiled periodically in the future, as they have been in the past, in an effort to resolve a fiscal crisis by artificial termination of the legal ceiling. This is a terrible waste of time. The debt ceiling as a fiscal tool is not just blunt and ineffective, but occasionally even mischievous.

Real fiscal action is corrective action, which is tough. Rather than accept responsibility for corrective change, many politicians would prefer to argue about economic assumptions. Have we assumed enough rate of growth? Have we assumed a high-enough inflation rate? Are we sure we have accurately computed the returns on taxes? Aren't we overestimating the cost of an aircraft carrier or a social welfare program? And so it goes, evasively. In fact, corrective action usually proves to be the only effective way to deal with fiscal policy.

As a former congressman, I can tell you that people are always writing to their legislators to say there ought to be another law to do this or to do that. They are always suggesting new ways in which government should be useful. Lots of times they will complain, by saying: "Why don't you cut back on spending?" In the same letter, they may add, "There ought to be a law requiring this additional government service that we have in mind," as if the money came from Canada or Utopia, or somewhere. If a polltaker asked them the right questions, they undoubtedly would say there are too many laws already and government spends too much. However, when programs and spending are near and dear to them, they seem to have no problem urging elected representatives to pass certain laws and enhance certain programs.

People do want government to be a problem solver, and as long as problem solving is going to be part of the role of government, this is going to cost money. The result is that there have been a whole bunch of panaceas that have come down the pike aimed at resolving fiscal problems in the easiest possible way. Understandably, a characteristic of members of Congress is to welcome such things. They are looking for ways to avoid tough steps they know they will otherwise have to take. The Budget Reform Act was considered one such panacea. Members would say to one another: "If we could just have our own congressional budget, a fiscal yardstick of our own instead of that presidential fiscal yardstick, the president's budget, we would be much better off." Ignoring the president's budget was easy, anyway. "If we could get one of our own," we would say, "even if it is less perfect than the one put together by OMB (the Office of Management and Budget), then at least we'd support our own measure of discipline and priority setting."

Well, the Budget Reform Act was enacted and though it is still in existence, it hasn't really changed the fiscal equation very much. As a matter of fact, looking at the end product shows that the deficit is much larger now than it was before that act was implemented. Legislative priorities, it appears, are as easy to ignore as presidential priorities.

There were other things in the past that were suggested as panaceas. Remember Bert Lance, President Carter's OMB director? He was in favor of zero-based budgeting. That was going to save us. We would go back and look at every item of appropriation, and every year we would attempt to justify the whole program from its inception, not just the increment beyond that which was spent in the previous year. We would not just say to a federal agency that might be seeking more money: "All right, you spent X-billion last year. This year, how much do you need to maintain the same program in the same way?" We would go back and try to rejustify the whole venture. That was going to save us from ourselves. The practice of zero-based budgeting lasted about a year.

Then along came the sunset law idea. Do you remember sunset laws? They were going to save us, too. Instead of enacting programs in perpetuity, we were going to enact them for only three or four years. At the end of those three or four years there would be an automatic total review. We would look back and see if a program had really accomplished what was expected. Sunset laws were also supposed to save us, fiscally, in the long run. The trouble is that when we looked at programs, upon the expiration of the time limits imposed, we found ourselves tempted to "improve" them, which cost more money.

The latest is, of course, the Gramm-Rudman-Hollings Law, which forces automatic cuts in governmental agencies and programs if Congress fails to do the same thing legislatively. Well, G-R-H has served a purpose, but it has not really solved the fundamental problem. Witness the so-called summit agreement reached by congressional and administration leaders late in 1987. The pact called for savings and a little revenue raising totalling an estimated $23 billion. At best, this was truly a modest effort, providing no long-range answers and a bare bones bailout of a near-term fiscal crisis.

Well, Americans have learned, over a long and painful period of time, that panaceas really don't make much difference. They are merely tools that government might use. They may help, but they will not solve big problems. You can have the best hoe in the world and you still will have a weedy garden if you don't use the hoe effectively. The tools of government simply cannot take the place, we have found, of the will to govern. Tough decisions still have to be made to have a fiscal policy that is acceptable in the long run, if a functioning economy is what's wanted. No formula can avoid that necessity.

People ask, with reason, why should there be a concern about deficits, generally? A standard response is that a deficit is the end product of faulty fiscal policy. If you don't have income and outgo in the same fiscal ballpark, that means you are running up the national debt. I must say, there are some economists now who do not worry about the debt, even though it currently amounts to some $2 trillion. Now, I don't ask you to count all the digits in that $2 trillion-dollar figure, but our resources are going to have to be able to service that debt. In order to pay the service on it, to persuade people to continue to buy government bonds, and to pay them for lending their funds to the government, a lot of money is required— money that could be used on current services, instead of on a "dead horse."

I think most people understand (1) that a large national debt and a growing debt service do impinge on the government's ability to do things in the present, and (2) that to the extent we pass both burdens on to future generations, they will be handicapped, too. By not paying fully now for our own government services, we Americans clearly will not help our children accomplish what they want to accomplish with the taxes they will pay. They won't be satisfied simply trying to maintain a magnificent debt cost for what their ancestors have already enjoyed.

A national debt and a growing deficit are not necessarily fatal, of course, unless over a period of time, the debt grows faster than the economy. I really don't expect the national debt to be entirely paid off. If the debt can be maintained, though, in a rough relation to the national economy as a whole, Americans can stay out of serious trouble. If we don't, if we leave alone, let's say, a deficit near $200 billion, and let it grow, then every year that deficit will be contributing another $20 billion or so to the debt service necessary to maintain the debt. The $20 billion will go up gradually as the amount compounds. And if that amount starts climbing at a faster rate than the economy is growing, we are sooner or later going to arrive at the point where, in order to meet the obligations of the debt service, we will have to print more money. In other words, what we would wind up doing at the end of a period of fiscal debauchery is to try to make the debt meaningless by making money meaningless.

Now, what's wrong with that? Why can't we just start from scratch again? The problem is that in the process we would use up all the savings of the American people. The people who have been asked to contribute to social security, the people who have paid (or had paid in their behalf) a lot of money into pension funds, the people who have set money aside in the bank, all these people would find that since money has become meaningless, their effort at self-sufficiency has been totally frustrated, and at that point something bad would happen to our democracy. What we face today is not a happy situation. I don't want to belabor the point. If we are going to talk about getting and spending, we have to talk about the need for fiscal discipline, the need for a corrective.

CONTROLS: AUTOMATIC AND AD HOC

Earlier, I suggested that the fiscal crisis of today is a little more complicated as a result of a change in the tax law, made in 1981, that established indexation of the income tax (tying brackets to cost-of-living advances). You may recall my central point, which is that, prior to indexing, increasing inflation caused increasing tax rates to the nominal amount of money that people received. Even if they weren't getting increased purchasing power, even if they weren't getting real money back in the same degree that they had in previous years, the government would take a bigger cut in taxes collected because the taxpayer would have moved into a higher bracket. I described that as bracket creep.

During the 1970s, particularly, bracket creep brought into the Treasury as much as an estimated $60 billion dollars a year to finance growth, or to keep the deficit down. Knowing that additional, automatic tax increase money was coming in, federal estimators could look into the future and create rosy projection graphs. They knew that revenue would rise as progressive taxation was impacted by inflation, and they assumed that expenditures would be kept under control. Therefore, there would be, at some point out in the future, a balanced budget. No longer is that game possible. Income taxes are indexed and this means that in order to bring about a balanced budget, Congress will have to take affirmative action, the corrective action I said was tough. Americans cannot count any longer on those automatic increases in revenues. So, politicians find themselves bemused by a deficit that seems to go on and on indefinitely, rather than being automatically reduced by bracket creep.

In looking at the fiscal equation, there are always two sides, as there are on all equations. Generally, spending (not taxation) determines the size of the burden on people, because government borrowing comes out of the people, too. The government pays what it needs to pay in order to get the money it needs to borrow. It has the first crack at the savings of the American people, or the savings of foreigners, now that so much foreign money is coming into this country. Foreigners, because of their investment in this country, are helping Americans to reduce our deficit. We can't count on them to continue doing that, and we should not count on them, but the truth is that they have actually helped us a great deal by providing the wherewithal to meet our deficit in recent years. However, borrowing the government undertakes in order to deal with the deficit usurps savings and economic resources, which otherwise could be used in the private sector for risk-taking that helps to create jobs and move our economy ahead. Therefore, that borrowing comes out of the people, too.

What Americans spend, then, determines the total burden on the people, because borrowing comes out of people's savings just as taxes come out of their income or their savings. Obviously, if spending is not caught and controlled, sooner or later revenues will have to go up. The current opposition of the current president to increased revenues is not going to change that reality. Maybe he says: "Not on my watch," and means it, but unless spending is controlled, there is no alternative because the burden is constantly increasing. The runaway growth of the deficit may change the economy, and this may indicate that appropriateness of changes in the incidence of taxation. That is, you may want to juggle the tax system so that this or that element will pay a bigger share than it is paying now. Generally, though, tax policy is going to be driven by spending policy.

In the preceding discussion, I talked about tax bills of the past. I noted that there were situations when scandals developed because some observers perceived that loopholes were being used excessively, that various entities outside congress would steer Americans toward a tax reform bill that would improve the fairness of the system. Government representatives "bought" those tax changes, usually by concurrently giving a tax cut, thus feeding the idea that tax reform would reduce people's taxes. The 1981 tax act cut back on the taxes of everybody by 25 percent over a three-year period, and, in fact, reduced total taxes significantly as part of that reform. After that, I remember saying to people that you can memorize this tax law because we aren't going to be able to afford another one for a long time, and that was because I thought at the time that tax reform would always have to be bought.

Since then, however, tax reform has not been so much a striving for equity, or the perception of equity, as it has been a response to a perceived need for funds. In TEFRA (the 1982 act) and in DEFRA (the 1984 act), the driving force was not really a desire for structural change to alter the incidence of taxation, to relieve the burden on specific people and impose it on others. The purpose was to try to raise a little more money because the deficit was bothering us. We didn't raise much and the technique we used in TEFRA and the 1984 act was again the elimination of preferences. These were special provisions in the tax law that take some socially desirable goal and reduce taxes on operations that advance that goal.

In other words, the 1982 act and the 1984 act were primarily efforts to raise money through elimination of preferences. They were not like the "old line" tax reforms that involved the purchase, to some degree, of desired structural change. Since they were efforts to raise money, this president basically didn't like them. He supported them and asked for them because he still felt nervous about the deficit at that point. Yet, he did not enjoy the process because it involved modest increases in taxes paid by those people whose preferences had been eliminated or reduced. That's a major reason why the president liked the 1986 reform bill and why it passed both House and Senate. It was billed essentially as a tax reduction measure because of its sharp cuts in top marginal rates. It was consistent with the 1982 and 1984 bills in that it removed preferences (this time around, in wholesale lots), but these provisions were overshadowed by lower marginal rates.

Now, let me go back briefly to spending, the other side of the fiscal equation. Dealing with the equation is complicated by the extent to which Congress is a human institution. Old-line conservatives say: "We are not really in favor of a tax increase because we know from past experience and from dealing with Congress as a human institution that if they raise taxes, they will feel they can then afford to spend more money." That is, indeed, to some degree characteristic of people's representatives. Having taken tough action by raising taxes, a member of Congress is very likely to feel that this removes pressure from the spending side, and many people think that concern about this kind of thinking is part of the psychology of Ronald Reagan.

Is the president, in David Stockman's words, trying to starve the tumor of government? He does not view government favorably. He may think the way to starve the tumor of government is not to feed it. I'd feel a lot better about this if we didn't have such a big deficit. We're just kidding ourselves if we're borrowing to maintain big government instead of taxing to maintain it.

TAX EXPENDITURES: THEORY AND FACT

That brings me to something that must become a part of the discussion. It's called the tax expenditure theory. There was a professor from Harvard, a brilliant man by the name of Stanley Surrey, mentioned earlier, who had very strong theories of tax reform. He believed the tax system should be used solely for raising money, not as a tool to express any social purposes through granting preferences of one sort or another. He wanted, in short, to do away with all preferences, which he termed tax expenditures.

Preferences are—as I have described them—a form of problem solving. They are a way to encourage, through incentives, some investment by the private sector in areas for which Congress is unwilling to appropriate money. One of the interesting questions is: "Are preferences desirable for that purpose?" Are they more desirable or less desirable than creating a public program to solve a problem and then appropriating tax collections directly to deal with the problem?

Obviously, there are two ways to spend money if following a belief in the tax expenditure theory. Any preference that is granted costs the government money because it reduces to the extent of the preference any revenue coming in through the tax system. If Congress really controlled spending, if it truly placed a lid on spending, a lot of people would be introducing bills to authorize tax preferences of one sort or another. The dome of the Capitol would overflow with tax preference bills designed to get private money into problem solving processes, if it were no longer possible to get it through appropriations because of real controls on spending.

There are situations where preferences are more desirable than public programs to solve problems. What are those situations? They exist where there is a need for more than the usual stability because planning is involved. For instance, there are preferences for business that exist in order to encourage capital investment. Most people, I think, believe these necessary in a world economy in which other countries have different types of subsidies or direct public expenditure to feed economic activity. Most business planning goes on over a long period of time. A long time is needed to plan a new factory, and if business leaders were entirely reliant on annual appropriation processes for their resources, quite frankly a lot of that risk-taking never would occur. Tax preferences are harder to change than annual, direct appropriations, and, therefore, a long-term business investor considers them a more stable incentive on which to rely. I should note at this point that while the above observation is, I believe, accurate, it has been considerably weakened by a recent congressional propensity for tinkering with tax laws in virtually every Congress.

Another example of the wise use of a preference has to do with charity. If we relied for the survival of charity on appropriation processes, it is one of those things that probably would go out the window pretty fast during a time of fiscal crisis. Centralized problem solving, through government programs, is not very flexible. A preference for charitable contributions adds to the pluralism of a responsive society. Also, a tax preference is voluntary; no one has to use it. People do have to pay taxes, which is the way Congress gets money for direct appropriations, anyway. Preferences are more acceptable in a democracy because of this element of choice, which isn't characteristic of government programs.

There are disadvantages to tax preferences, also. Many people will say this is a less efficient way to "problem-solve." Predicting revenue loss is very difficult as a result of granting a preference because money can't be targeted to the same degree as if an appropriation is made and sent specifically in one direction. I remember that Walter Reuther, the well-known, late, labor leader, who came before our committee years ago, said that he didn't want any more preferences because, while designed to benefit the poor, in most cases, the poor get crumbs and the rich get loaves. Well, that's one of the problems about preferences. If they are in the law, anybody who wants to claim them has the right to do so. They are worth more to a taxpayer in a high bracket than to one in a lower bracket. Preferences make the tax law more complicated. If the tax is just a simple tax for collection purposes, that's all there is to it; everyone has to pay those taxes. By putting preferences in the law to deal with problems for which the government was unwilling to appropriate money, the tax law is greatly complicated.

The very term "tax expenditure" sometimes draws this kind of negative reaction: "What an outrage to say that anything you don't tax away from the people is a tax expenditure." Lots of conservatives use that phraseology, but one difficulty is that some people opposing the tax expenditure theory of Professor Surrey's believe that any preference is justified if it substitutes for direct spending. Get rid of a particular government program and just take care of it with a tax credit, some will argue, regardless of whether the government program is appropriate or whether it is an appropriate area for government problem solving in the first place. Despite all this, there is a growing consensus that preferences should be eliminated. The problem, then, is what preferences should be eliminated? One of the interesting allegations recurring in tax policy debates is that those preferences that are eliminated are chosen by arithmetic, not because they are archaic or otherwise inappropriate.

If tax policy leaders decide, as they have done in major bills of the 1980s, especially in the 1986 act, that preferences should go, the next question is: "In what order?" It has been my notion that preferences that are scheduled for elimination should fall into three categories. First, those that benefit the few rather than the many should go. If a preference benefits only a limited number of people, that's not a good way or a fair way to solve problems, or so that argument goes. If it benefits a few rich people, obviously it is not a very satisfactory preference in terms of democracy. Second, eliminate those preferences that are mainly of an historical nature. Get rid of those put into law years ago that may not be relevant to a changing economy. There are such preferences. They never would be enacted today if we were to start from scratch. But because people have come to accept them as an integral part of the tax code, they continue, even though they are not terribly relevant to the functioning of today's economy. The third type of preference that many people say should be eliminated is the kind that actually distorts the economy and causes capital flows to move in other than economic directions. An example cited is the accelerated depreciation schedule for commercial buildings. Many people believe that we built far too many extra feet of office space in Houston, Dallas, New York City, and other parts of the United States because tax preferences benefited commercial real estate. This has placed capital, the argument says, which should be available for other purposes, into useless office space that is not occupied. That space is not economically justified, but is built for tax purposes only, or so goes the claim. The claim was upheld clearly in the 1986 Tax Reform Act, which clamped down hard, for example, on passive loss rules as they apply to real estate.

Other major preferences that were eliminated in the 1986 tax reform bill were reduction of accelerated depreciation, and the elimination of investment tax credit. Those changes, I am convinced, were chosen because they would raise a lot of money. The driving force in these cases was revenue, more than tax policy. The investment tax credit repeal and decelerated depreciation were estimated to raise over $119 billion, with which one could—and Congress did—buy significant rate reduction.

A major revenue raiser that was proposed, but not adopted in full, was repealing deductibility of state and local taxes. I realize that I must be suspect on such an issue because I come from New York, a high-tax state. This has been identified altogether too much, in my view, as a state issue, a New York State issue. I tend to be a decentralist; I am a Jeffersonian Republican. I believe in decentralization to the greatest degree possible and so, philosophically, I don't like the idea of increasing the cost of state and local government to state and local taxpayers. Inevitably, results will be reduction in services provided by state and local government, tempting the federal government to fill the vacuum. So I am glad the new law stopped short on this point, even though repeal was not turned back for philosophical reasons, but because the deduction was extremely popular.

Now, repeal of the ITC is another matter. I must say that farmers and other entrepreneurs do not like that one. Many farmers have lived on this investment tax credit because they have to make a lot of capital investment and they can offset 10 percent of this cost in the year purchases are made. Although I am not enamored of the investment tax credit, preferring instead a rapid write-off of the same capital items, I do believe it should be made permanent if incorporated into the law. Those likely to use the ITC are also likely to require long-range planning for major projects. For example, a steel firm intending to build a new mill should know well in advance whether the ITC will be available when needed machinery and other equipment are to be purchased. So the ITC should be something a taxpayer can count on; it should not be put into the law to stimulate the economy one year, then pulled out two years later because the economy has recovered. As John Byrnes put it back in the 1960s and 1970s, the ITC should not become an economic yo-yo.

Reformers generally have a choice of two possible approaches toward preferences. They can move incrementally to abolish preferences one at a time or they can move radically to try to get rid of a lot at once. The president decided that radical tax reform was what he wanted. If done all at once, he reasoned, prediction can be made about trade-offs. Eliminating many preferences simultaneously raises enough money to buy real rate reduction. He supported TEFRA and DEFRA, as I said, but didn't like them. He saw those acts as resulting in incremental tax increases because, in elimination of preferences, taxes rose on those who previously enjoyed the preferences. So he said, in effect, "let's do it all at once and balance unhappy effects with benefits of rate reduction."

Some Reagan watchers guessed that because the president really dislikes taxes and government, he saw great advantages in a simpler system, without preferences. A simpler tax would promote real resistance to raising tax rates in the future, since everyone will know how he or she is personally affected. Politically, raising taxes is easier through elimination of preferences. Everyone doesn't use preferences, but everyone is affected by rate increases. Was this what President Reagan was trying to do all along, get a simpler tax system so that everyone will oppose tax increases in the future? Well, you'll have to judge that yourself. I don't know whether that's been the president's motivation, but no politician is apt to do anything for just one reason. He may have had that in mind, but I would not be sure.

SOME THOUGHTS ON REVENUE NEUTRALITY

The new tax law obviously doesn't have a great deal to do with our current fiscal crisis. The legislation was revenue neutral, and its economic effects will not really be felt for some time. It was designed for revenue neutrality first by Don Regan, when he was treasury secretary, and then by Jim Baker, the next secretary, and by Dan Rostenkowski, chairman of Ways and Means. Revenue neutrality meant a different thing to "Rosty" than it did to the president. To the president it meant there will be no tax increase. To "Rosty" it meant there will be no tax reduction.

As to the future, how does anyone really know if the 1986 act is going to remain revenue neutral? All estimations are made over a five-year period. Now, I must tell you that most economists don't know what's going to happen next Tuesday, much less what's going to happen over a five-year period. One reality of tax law is that the amount of money that comes in is much more affected by the current economy at the time the tax is levied than it is by any jiggling that affects the structure of the tax law. No one really can tell how much money a change in the tax law is likely to produce without knowing also the state of the economy when that change becomes effective. A changing economy is a moving target, shifting the incidence of taxation, and nobody really understands whether true revenue neutrality is possible or not over the long haul.

Another interesting point, one which never seems to get discussed, is that there is a difference between revenue neutrality and budget neutrality. Remember that preferences are problem solvers. If there is a total government program to try to deal with problems affecting people, and preferences are eliminated, then if the same government involvement exists in that problem thereafter, there really should be replacement of it with an increased appropriation of some sort. Budget neutrality, therefore, may be considerably more expensive than elimination of the preference. To be sure to get the same effect, appropriation of more money or a retreat from the problem solving business may be necessary. So, that's another element to be considered when looking at revenue neutrality. Of course, President Reagan wanted to get government out of the problem-solving business, and so he perhaps didn't worry about budget neutrality.

As indicated earlier, people concerned about the deficit who assume a tax increase is necessary and desirable may also believe somehow that the 1986 act was an important preliminary to dealing with the fiscal problem. They seem to think that now that marginal rates are fewer and lower and the tax system is more acceptable to the American people via reforms that have been effected, there will be a tax rate increase to reduce the deficit. That, indeed, is one reason so many people are skeptical about the new tax law. Those who appear to be winners under the latest reform are doubtful they will be the winners for long.

There are many other things that can be said about the latest reform effort. I do find fascinating the result that simplification is no longer talked about in connection with the 1986 exercise, because the process of compromise so greatly complicated matters and distracted people who initially thought simplification was the whole reason for the exercise. I do believe that simplification is a siren song and that the siren has stopped wailing—at least for the time being. It is a siren song because, in a complex economy, it is not likely that a simple tax ultimately would be viewed as very fair, and the real effect of radical simplification is to transfer taxing authority from the legislative to the executive branch via the regulation route.

That is the sum of my message on getting and spending. It is, I think, important that Americans consider one other aspect of tax policy. This is the prime subject of this entire discussion's focus, which is how representative government deals with the process of taxation. I maintain that there are certain inherent characteristics of representative government that make such issues difficult ones with which to deal. Being realistic about that is important.

CHAPTER 6

TAXATION WITH REPRESENTATION: A CURRENT APPRAISAL

REPRESENTATIVE GOVERNMENT is a subject that, to say the least about it, no longer has the bloom of youth. Its relationship with taxation reeks of tension and trauma, as well as the mold of age. Samuel Johnson was credited with saying, in his usual wise way: "To tax and be loved or to love and be wise are not given to mortal man." We all remember that taxation without representation was a rallying cry for the very beginning of this nation, and today taxation remains, I believe, the most sensitive issue between the government and the people.

I already have mentioned that every year in Congress a large number of bills dealing with taxation in one way or another are filed. President Reagan has divined, and I believe quite correctly, that people do not enjoy working for the government through the tax system and are anxious to believe ill of it, if at all possible. They may have representation, but their own attitude toward taxation still ranges between wariness and hostility. Against that background, I would like to explore what taxation with representation means, since taxation without representation was considered a reasonable cause of the American Revolution.

First of all, representation has to be defined. It is obviously not leadership. I believe our system of government depends very heavily on leadership of the executive branch, and most representatives in Congress believe that, too. They further believe that their role is not to get too far out front, way ahead of the crowd. The issue of representation assumes input from outside, but we have had lots of talk over the years about how much better Congress would be if members, particularly of the House of Representatives, had longer terms, so that they could have more time to become expert. Members, however, do not really believe expertise is their function. Most of them believe that, as representatives, they are supposed to bring a citizen's view to government. They think of the House of Representatives as the ultimate expression of a citizen's responsibility.

Those of us who watch Congress with interest in it as an institution have noticed that people who come there with specific skills and specific interests tend to become vulnerable to the logrolling and back scratching that is part of the congressional scene. For their interests to remain too concentrated is not necessarily a good thing.

Successful congressional representatives are usually generalists, skating across all subjects with a surface credibility, exercising not expert judgment, but a citizen's judgment on questions that are presented to them. This means they have to have expert advice when dealing with specific questions, like those of taxation. They must have input from skilled staff, from the executive branch with all its experts, from knowledgeable people of their districts, from academic institutions, from analysts, from economists, and all the various people concerned with taxation. So, representation assumes input from outside. It assumes that knowledgeable and involved people can get access. But can they? And to what extent should they?

Those are particularly relevant questions, and worth considering because there is always much publicity about special interests' impact on legislation, especially those represented by people hovering around the door of the Ways and Means

Committee. There has always been a sizeable block of social scientists who believe that if representative government could somehow be isolated, it would function better. This group deplores the fact that members of Congress continue to run for office from the moment they are elected. They discount the fact that because their terms are so short, members must run continually if they want to stay on the job. This kind of representation assumes that representatives have an obligation to let interested parties get access to them. Now, obviously, that access is imperfect. If you represent, say, 520,000 people, there would be some difficulty for every one of them to get access to you. Most people, of course, are not directly affected by what their representatives are doing at any given time. Therefore, the only thing that representative government does require, I think, is the opportunity of accessibility.

Representative government often operates in this sequence: Government and staff experts set up a series of suggestions as to what should be done, and members of Congress bring to bear citizens' views, saying: "Wait a minute. I don't think my people will go for that," or, "Okay. That sounds like something reasonable." In this sequence, if a proposal gets knocked down, somebody sets it up in the other alley.

When I left Congress some people may have assumed that I would be a practicing tax lawyer because I had been dealing with tax policy for so long. I do not, however, have a precise knowledge about tax law even now, because as a congressman I had been exercising only a generalized judgment about tax matters on issues delineated for me by experts. Representation assumes that a representative is not going to be a blank file, reading and counting his or her letters and saying: "I have received 321 letters for, and 317 against, so I must vote for." Representation assumes that personal judgment also is a representative's responsibility. It may be a citizen's judgment to be sure, but the representative is still going to have to exercise that judgment individually.

Most representatives are political animals who factor in all the elements provided by the array of so-called experts, by various other political leaders, by constituents, or at least the active groups among the constituents who are particularly affected by legislation. All those things are automatically taken into account by a political animal. In the final analysis, the representative is going to have to ask: "If a majority of my people knew as much about this issue as I know, now that the experts have explained it to me and now that the political environment has demanded some response from me, how would a majority of them vote?" That is what representation essentially comes down to. If the representative does not do what the majority would want most of the time, then the people have not only the right, but the duty, to replace the representative because representative government is not working.

COMPROMISE AND COMPLEXITY

Part of the cost of taxation with representation, as I have tried to make clear, is the complexity begat by compromise. I often think of that cost, recalling a specific episode back at the beginning of my congressional service. One morning, there arose in the Ways and Means Committee some very fine point of law that none of us understood, except perhaps John Byrnes and Wilbur Mills. The two of them—the chairman and the ranking Republican—started discussing this point at nine o'clock when the committee met. And they argued about it, from diametrically opposed positions, before their wide-eyed junior colleagues who didn't understand it in any respect, all morning. I remember that we went in frustration off for a lunch break when bells began ringing over on the floor of the House and we had to go there to vote on a pending matter. As we left the committee room, Wilbur turned to the Joint Tax Committee's chief of staff, that brilliant man named Larry Woodworth, saying: "Larry, you understand what John and I have been arguing about. Now go out there and work up a compromise for us." Larry reportedly stayed up most of the night and came in the next morning with eighty-two pages of finely-drawn compromise for all of us to read and digest. Even so, again, except for Mills and Byrnes, we did not fully and thoroughly understand it, and neither has anyone else from that time to this. There was a tremendous complexity on a very small point, because the compromise accommodated total disagreement.

That illustrated graphically for me that a big part of the cost of representation, since representatives tend to compromise diversity, is complexity. Compromise is about the only way to get a majority together. Different things are important to different people, so what is there to do when someone wants to produce a feasible, enactable legislative proposal? Compromise strings together enough of those things that are important to a wide range of people so that a sufficient number of them will support the resulting package, frequently building into the law a complexity that includes inconsistency. Interestingly enough, complexity, inconsistency, and the ultimate compromise will combine, I think, to continue focusing much attention on the so-called minimum tax.

The minimum tax emerged, as I mentioned, in the 1969 act. Again, the outrage of the day was that a few big fish were slipping through the net—the people that then Treasury Secretary Joe Barr designated as millionaires who paid no taxes. An obvious reaction would have been to get rid of preferences that were used in tandem to reduce those millionaires' taxes to zero. In most cases, however, those were popular preferences, so what was done instead was to come up with the idea of a minimum tax.

The Committee on Ways and Means said, in effect, to taxpayers: "We want you to continue to use preferences, but if you use them enough so that your tax falls below a certain portion of, or percentage of, your real income, we are going to tax you on the preferences, so that you will be paying at least some significant tax. In other words, we were not interested in fairness, we were interested in the perception of fairness." The overriding question was: "How do we avoid the publicity that will lead people to believe the tax system is unfair?" The problem was not how to get a full and fair quota of tax from these people, but how to insure that they pay something.

The minimum tax, in fact, is ambivalent. It lets people continue to use the preference incentive, but, if they use it a lot, they are going to be taxed accordingly. That is a compromise, a compromise to prevent bad appearance in the tax law, and I suspect it is going to be used again and again to raise revenue eroded by preference. Revision of both the individual and corporate minimum tax provisions became an important, revenue-producing part of the 1986 Tax Reform Act, and still further revision is being talked about in tax circles now.

In addition to intellectual confusion caused by such ambivalent devices as the minimum tax, members of Congress also find the tax law complicated because it was put together at different times for different purposes. Some years after enactment of a particular tax measure, which took place long before they arrived, new legislators (or old ones, for that matter) may not understand the philosophical considerations that generated a specific provision. The economy changes, politics change, public perceptions change, and even just one tough newspaper story may be enough to set Congress off on a whole series of legislative tangents. Over a period of time, the tax code itself becomes one massive discontinuity, and to understand it, one has to know when a section was put into it and what motivated the insertion. The whole is not permeated by a current spirit and motivation, and that is one of the reasons why representatives wind up supporting apparent inconsistency.

THE IRA EXPERIMENTS

Not only circumstances change, but theories change, and as an example of a theory that has had a lot of problems, and is still unresolved, I would cite the theory that gave rise to the so-called IRA, or Individual Retirement Account. The IRA was designed as a $2,000 annual deduction, if one had $2,000 of earned income that could be put into a bank or other form of savings and not thereafter removed at will. It was to be used for retirement purposes only, not to be drawn upon until the attainment of a certain age. The deduction gained in the year of investment was a valuable tax deferral. A tax was to be paid on the IRA amount only when the taxpayer started drawing it out. Premature withdrawals carry steep penalties.

The IRA was, then, a device to delay tax payment, by paying money into a sequestered account. Reportedly, it saved a number of thrift institutions, because they were subject to a terrible condition called "disintermediation." If interest rates go up, people take their money out of ordinary bank accounts where they can get a certain percentage of interest, and put it directly into higher interest paper. The bank finds itself losing liquidity as a result of the disintermediation. If, however, IRA money is put into a thrift institution, the thrift institution can count on having that money until the depositor reaches retirement age. Because of the huge early withdrawal penalty, most of these funds stay put.

The Committee on Ways and Means accepted IRAs in theory, originally, because we were concerned statistically. We were told that the private pension funds in commerce and industry were available only to 40 percent of America's working people. In other words, of the whole work force, only 40 percent got private pensions where they worked. Private pensions involve major deferral of tax; the money is invested for participants; they do not pay a tax on it when it goes into private pension funds or when the pension income accumulates. They pay a tax only when they draw it out later. In aggregate, this involves a very large total tax avoidance, because lots of big companies have big pension plans. It is a very expensive tax preference, based on the natural desire of most people for secure retirement, and on the competition for good employees. However, when told that only 40 percent really benefit from those private plans, the committee asked: "How can we spread the benefits of tax deferral to poorer people who don't have private pensions at work? Is a tax preference justified that benefits only 40 percent of the people? Don't the rest unfairly pay higher taxes because the preference reduces the taxable income of those with pensions?" Unless we were able to find some device of that sort, we thought we would not be justified in permitting continuance of private pension plans. So we set up the IRAs in the mid-seventies.

By 1980, we started to look at how many people were using IRAs, and we discovered that the answer was disappointingly few. Big companies with the private pension plans also paid the highest wages. The sad thing was that the very people who needed tax deferral for retirement purposes, and did not get it through their jobs, were also the people who got the lowest levels of pay. Since they were the poorest people, they were not in a position, as they saw it, to take advantage of the IRA deduction, or to set aside the money necessary to claim it.

Later, when Congress was passing the first Reagan tax reform bill, the Ways and Means Committee became deeply concerned about our very low national savings rate. The rate was between 3 and 5 percent, so the idea occurred: "Let's make IRAs also available to people who already have pensions at work." The theory had changed. We were no longer concerned about spreading tax preference to those who otherwise couldn't get it. They hadn't claimed it anyway. We decided to make IRAs available to those who would claim it, whether they needed it or not, to increase the national savings rate. As a result restrictions were relaxed and more IRAs were authorized. The people who had private pensions through their jobs also had more available savings money, and they liked the extra $2,000 tax deduction. Thus, the same people who had tax deferral through the private pension system now could augment that with IRAs.

By 1986, however, the Committee on Ways and Means and the Senate Finance Committee were taking another look at IRAs. Studies were showing that the expanded availability of IRAs had no discernible impact on the level of aggregate personal savings. Many employers had adopted qualified cash or deferred arrangements, allowing employees to make discretionary contributions providing them with tax-favored treatment essentially equivalent to that given IRA contributions. The committees decided that the wide availability of options, to make elective deferrals under cash or deferred arrangements and tax-sheltered annuities, overrode the earlier concern that individuals in employer-maintained plans should be able to save additional amounts for retirement on a discretionary basis. Studies also showed that IRA utilization was low among lower-income taxpayers who could be least likely to accumulate significant retirement savings in the absence of a specific tax provision.

The committees now believed that higher-income taxpayers would generally have saved in some other form, even without the tax deduction, and that substantially lower tax rates would eliminate the need for IRA deductions for higher-income taxpayers who participate in other tax-favored retirement plans. Thus, for higher-income taxpayers, the new law reinstates generally the rules prior to ERTA, which limit IRA deductions to those taxpayers who are not covered by an employer-provided pension plan. The 1986 Act permits all individuals, including higher-income taxpayers who are covered by an employer's retirement plan, to make nondeductible contributions to an IRA with a continued deferral of tax on the earnings on these nondeductible contributions. This is a compromise to dull the disappointment of those no longer able to claim the deduction.

Whether that remains the last word on IRAs, only time and changing economic conditions, plus taxpayer demands, will tell. The jury is still out, but I have not seen any data proving that IRAs have, in fact, created more savings rather than simply savings in a different form. The United States savings rate recently was estimated at about 4.8 percent, as opposed to West Germany's 15 percent, Canada's 11 percent, and Japan's 20 percent. In other words, our savings rate does not appear to have risen as much as was expected when IRAs were first enacted or expanded. Whatever happens to the whole IRA idea in the end, the IRA story does demonstrate, I think, how theories change and why the tax law winds up as a hodgepodge.

RANDOM AND OTHER INFLUENCES

Representative government sometimes changes the law quite casually, without study, because of an individual intervention by an obscure congressman. Let me tell you a story of how this once happened to me when I was a junior minority member of Ways and Means. After I had been in Congress for two years, I was appalled to discover how many files of correspondence I had accumulated. I asked what to do about it, and was told that many gave their records to the university from which they had been graduated. After I had shipped mine off to my alma mater, I was astonished to receive a professional appraisal for $2,200. When I asked about that, I was told it was for tax purposes, since I had made a donation to a charity. That didn't seem right, and I phoned the Washington office of IRS and asked them to send an agent to explain it to me. An avuncular agent, skilled at dealing with congressmen, arrived and told me the law was clear that those records, though gathered at the public expense, belonged to me to give, and he assured me that the $2,200 was the smallest such valuation he had ever seen. He told me Lyndon Johnson, whose returns he had prepared for years, had taken from the White House thousands of documents, which he would contribute to a charity over a number of post-presidential years to improve his tax position. I took the deduction, but it still didn't seem right. And as I talked about it with some of my colleagues, I began to see a pattern of abuse.

Some months later, when Ways and Means had completed work on the 1969 Tax Reform Act, my first big one, Chairman Mills asked, as we were about to wrap it up: "Has anyone anything else he wants to bring up?" It was an executive session, supposedly secret, and I told the committee of my experience, saying that it looked to me like a scandal waiting to happen. Mills saw my point immediately, and announced that he would have the committee decree that, as of that very day, such deductions of the value of public papers given to charity would be prohibited by the new law we were in the process of discussing. Some members in the room sputtered that they had not given their papers yet, but he remained firm, and I left the room feeling very righteous.

To my surprise, I was met at the door by a reporter from a national newspaper, who told me he wanted to know the source of my information about Lyndon Johnson. I was considerably taken aback initially, because I had just emerged from a closed meeting and wondered immediately how anyone could know so quickly what had taken place inside. In any event, afraid that I would get my friend, the avuncular IRS agent, fired, I refused to tell him, and the reporter said he'd "get" me for not cooperating with him. Two days later his paper published a big article about this little known loophole, which it noted I had claimed because of my inside information as a legislator. I got poison-pen letters from all over.

The change stayed in the law, and later Mills attributed it publicly to me, which led to my receiving even more poison-pen letters, this time from universities and libraries, in every part of the United States, because they were losing the tax incentive that encouraged public officials to give their public papers to such institutions for research purposes. Even more embarrassing, President Nixon or his agents supposedly caused the deed of trust of his public papers to be backdated to a day before the fatal day of my intervention, and that backdating became a minor incident later in the Watergate scandal because allegations were made that Nixon improperly claimed the tax deduction after the change in the law. I hadn't even planned this change. No one was forewarned, yet in many circles my name was mud. I don't pretend this is typical of how laws get changed, but it does illustrate that things sometimes mysteriously appear in the tax laws without pre-meditation—a freak of representative government.

Many people worry about representative government's dealing with taxation because they hear so much about the probability of corruption in the process. I must acknowledge that there are an awful lot more lobbyists in Washington than there were when I first went there, a little more than two decades ago. At that time, business communities spoke to Congress largely through "cap" organizations, such as the Chamber of Commerce, the National Association of Manufacturers, the Business Round Table, and the National Federation of Independent Business. Over the years, those groups have become increasingly inclusive and diverse. They probably find great difficulty in speaking with one voice now. They have constituency problems of their own.

Many people and groups, during the sixties and seventies, sent representatives to Washington because of their great concern over the high degree of business regulation that characterized that period. The result was that many lobbyists in Washington were there not because of tax concerns; they were there because of regulation concerns. Some business leaders felt they could be better represented on the scene as a specific industry, and not through trade associations or major business organizations. So, many representatives who were sent there have not come home even though there has been a lot of deregulation. Some of these Washington "reps" have shifted over and are now part of the lobbying crowd worrying about taxes. At the same time, there has been growth of the political action committee, or PAC, movement. Political action committees were adopted in wholesale fashion during the seventies. Many businesses set up PACs, which contribute heavily to election campaign funds. They tend to contribute particularly to incumbents and many business people tend to view PAC contributions as access money.

Combine the two—extra lobbyists and the large amounts of money that PACs have to distribute—and you have a growing perception that special interests are buying their way into special representation on tax matters. Clearly, running for office nowadays costs a lot of money. The average contested race involves a congressman's spending as much as $250,000 on a campaign. That is only an average. Sometimes as much as a million dollars, or even several million, will be spent for a job that pays considerably less than $100,000. Therefore, a lot of money changes hands in the process of someone's trying to get enough to run effectively. The environment for decision-making has changed. For example, I already have discussed the opening of committee meetings and conferences, with the result that the lobbyists are right there in the front of the committee room, watching, gimlet-eyed, the decision makers.

However, despite horror stories in the press on this subject, I do not believe that the actual existence of corruption to that extent, the buying of votes on tax legislation, is a prevalent condition. I do recall vividly one episode, though, that was extremely illuminating in this regard. It involved a well-known Western millionaire who had bought a brokerage business in New York and lost a lot of money. He was unable to carry over his losses for tax purposes for more than a few years and the result was that he was not able fully to offset them against his other income. He hired a former commissioner of the IRS, a very well-known, liberal, Democratic lawyer in Washington, and they set about trying to get an amendment passed that would allow operating loss carry-overs to be deductible for a greater number of years. The lawyer went to Phil Landrum, a member of the Ways and Means Committee, a Democrat from Georgia, and a well-known and distinguished man, and got him to sponsor the amendment. The amendment made sense. It simply treated individuals the way corporations were treated as far as loss carry-overs were concerned. Without getting into the technical details of either the amendment or loss carry-overs, let's say that the amendment was a fairly sensible arrangement.

The committee considered the amendment on a routine basis. Thirteen of the twenty-five-man committee supported it and twelve opposed it. A very good investigative reporter from the *Wall Street Journal* started looking into it. Before we knew it, there was an article in the *Journal* pointing out that of the thirteen who voted for this change in the law, eleven had received contributions of at least a thousand dollars (a few of them after the election that preceded this action by a few months) from the same man who was now seeking to benefit from the change in the law. Three members of the Ways and Means Committee, two Republicans and a Democrat, were defeated, at least partly as a result of that story in the *Wall Street Journal*.

As it happened, I voted for the amendment, but because I had made it an ironclad rule to accept no more than fifty dollars from any single source in any of my campaigns, I had no worry about appearing to have sold my vote. I still thought the change was sensible, and I did not reverse my vote, although a number of my colleagues did, because of appearances, and I can understand very well why they did so. I am personally convinced that no one, except perhaps Phil Landrum, knew that this particular millionaire was involved in the issue from the start. An irrefutable law of political life, though, is that what people think is what is real in a democracy, and in this case they thought the money given by the millionaire had resulted in the vote. Of course, the committee played into their hands by responding guiltily and reversing the vote. You do have to worry about appearances in representative government.

What is the reality? Harold Ickes was Franklin Roosevelt's Secretary of the Interior, and was known popularly as a curmudgeonly sort of fellow. There is a story that one day he was approached by a young congressman who asked: "What should I do? I'm getting all these offers from special interests involved in the work of my committee?" I will not repeat the exact response, which was a little scabrous. But Harold said in effect: "Young man, if you can't take their money, drink their booze, and then vote against them, you don't belong here."

My impression is that most of my colleagues are perfectly capable of taking money from PACs representing special interests—trade associations, labor unions, ideological groups, et cetera—because they see that as part of the system under which they have to raise money for election purposes. In many cases, they take money from both sides of a political or economic equation, from labor and business, or from both sides of an ideological argument, and, anyway, they try to maintain a degree of objectivity. I do think that support of representative government and a belief by the people that it is functioning in the general interest and not in behalf of special interests is terribly important. So I would like to find ways within the Constitution to reduce the amount of money required in elections and ways of controlling the way money is given.

I think that what is almost as damaging as the perception of large PAC contributions is the Washington cocktail party, which goes on all the time. Members of the Ways and Means Committee and other members of Congress have fund raisers to which they invite lobbyists for, say, $500 a ticket. As immaculate a man as John Kenneth Galbraith, the noted economist, told me that he had first met Lyndon Johnson in 1938, when Galbraith agreed to be a host at a Washington cocktail party designed to introduce Lyndon to the oil community in Washington. The future president was looking for campaign money. So this is not a new issue. I personally believe that most congressmen are honest, and I wish the appearances were more attractive.

In sum, I tend to put down the possibility of real corruption, although the mere perception of scandal probably is as serious for representative government as scandal itself. Having served in Congress for twenty years, I have a good deal of confidence in the integrity of the average congressman. However, I acknowledge that there is a problem for representative government in dealing with as sensitive an issue as taxation, in light of the committee members' constant involvement in money raising and related activities.

AN INSTITUTION ALWAYS BEHIND THE CURVE

Now, however, I should discuss, at least a little, the inherent laggard qualities of representative government. Representatives, as I said earlier, wait for a consensus, or a crisis, or for strong, executive leadership. They do not necessarily consider themselves leaders. I think that for us all to decide whether we want leadership or representation is important. Whether talking about taxes or any other complex issue that faces modern society, representatives of the people tend to emphasize responsiveness and not leadership. Congressmen pride themselves on the fact that they do, ultimately, what the people want. To be sure of what the people want, they may wait for either heat-shielding executive leadership, a crisis, or at least a perceived consensus among the people. All this means that everybody else is likely to decide what is needed before Congress decides. Congress is inherently behind the curve on the decision-making process.

It is interesting that President Johnson's Great Society was based on the idea that government would lead Americans into a new and better way of national life. Since then, the government has been dragging its heels. It may have pretended to solve those same problems Johnson saw, but generally it has waited. It often waits in a fiscal crisis, until a consensus emerges to support tough action. This is not an efficient way to do business, especially the nation's business. Those people who believe that government should be efficient are very frustrated. The other side of the coin is that the current practice doesn't carry the risks of power abuse.

Our founding fathers built right into the American representative system a high degree of impasse. I would be the first to acknowledge that we do not have the bucolic arcadia of Thomas Jefferson's time, which permits government to drag its feet or even doze off on the way to decision making. There are real dangers inherent in the inefficiency of our decision-making process in this modern "high tech" world. There are, though, good things that still can be said about it. A leading alternative form of government for free people is a parliamentary system, and there are those who advocate it, particularly those who have served with unsuccessful presidents. The parliamentary system offers an instant alternative instead of a system of checks and balances. It permits quick decision making. If the British government were to have submitted a tax bill as President Reagan did, it would have been passed the next day in Parliament, not two years later. If that tax bill proved in practice to be terribly unpopular, a vote of no confidence would result in a new government. This is a zigzag type of government approach that would reverse the process, rather than hammer it out through a long and torturous process of compromise, as we in America do.

Business people used to come into my office when I was a congressman, and when I tried to tell them all this they would say: "That is an outrage. We sent you down here to solve our problems. Now solve them!" I could understand their frustration, because they were used to making decisions and immediately implementing them. I would say to them: "Do you really want a government that moves so efficiently that it can do for the people what the people aren't ready to have done for them?" Usually they would reply: "Yes. Do it right. Do it now." I would ask them who they thought would make the decision, and they would say: "Oh, you crummy politicians! Of course, you'll do it all wrong." It is this kind of irony that our system engenders.

If philosopher kings could be identified, and given the power to do what is right, then going through this cumbersome democratic procedure wouldn't be necessary; we could avoid this slowness, this impasse-creating, this compromise-inducing system. The philosopher king could anticipate a crisis. Such a person could solve the deficit, for example, before it caused pain and suffering, before the correction became pro-cyclical instead of counter-cyclical. The philosopher king has, however, been one of the great mirages of history. The problem is that people have learned, if they have studied history, that systems usually do not last very long if they are based on the assumption that kings would be philosophers. Such rulers usually wind up much more as kings than as philosophers. I think a pretty good case can be made for Americans being a free people because we are skeptical of government and because we want its powers hedged and defused and brought together with difficulty. We put our trust, instead, in ourselves, and in the various voluntary agencies that are spread throughout our society to provide responsive problem solving. We understand that our destinies are not safely turned over to governments that are distant and inaccessible. We understand that we are usually better off if we try to use self-reliance.

I suppose that is what our American democracy is going to be like as long as we are a free people. This process of self-governing is not gratifying, because it is not easy. It is not gratifying, because it is not efficient. But it is gratifying because, ultimately, it is concerned about what we, the people, think. It is gratifying, because, ultimately, we are able, by representative government, to govern ourselves.

INDEX

Y

CLASSIC

Date _6 - 2005_

Initials _cjw - BBfAL_

Initials _____